Advance Praise for

This deeply biblical, theological, ar
worship offers powerful guidance tc
lenges of unsettled worship patterns and traditions. Writing out of his own
experience as a leader of worship through this time of pandemic, Justin
Bishop re-imagines what it means to be the worshiping people of God in a
virtual age. *Sensing God Online* is the most significant book that any church
leader or minister will read in the coming year as they seek to bridge the
gap between a gathered community glad to be back in the sanctuary and a
scattered one content with virtual worship in its own sacred space beyond
those walls.

—*Robert N. Nash, Jr.*
Arnall-Mann-Thomasson Professor of Mission and Comparative Religions
McAfee School of Theology, Mercer University

While the COVID-19 pandemic's lasting effects for local congregations
may not be fully realized for years, Justin Bishop's prescient thinking and
praxis about worship during this new era should be carefully considered
and quickly implemented. Bishop's call for congregations and leaders to
shift from transliterated worship to translated worship should shake all
our preconceptions about returning worship to "normal" as things were
in pre-COVID days. *Sensing God Online* combines sturdy scholarship and
wisdom with practical and real-world advice for all who seek to lead congregations and individuals in offering their best selves in worship to God.

—*Rev. Jody Long*
Executive Coordinator
Cooperative Baptist Fellowship of Georgia

When the COVID pandemic hit in 2020, the ground shifted underneath
most churches in America. For congregations that were accustomed to
gathering at church for worship each Sunday, the pandemic put an end to
in-person worship. Most of these congregations resorted to some form of
online worship, but learning to use technology while planning meaningful
worship experiences proved to be a huge learning curve. Justin Bishop offers
practical help for these times by demonstrating how to use technology in
creative ways that can appeal to the senses, emotions, and intellect of online
worshipers. With theological and biblical awareness, Justin claims that

online worship can indeed offer a sacred encounter with God. This book is a must-read for all churches who desire to do online worship with quality, integrity, and creativity.

—*Karen Massey, Associate Dean*
McAfee School of Theology, Mercer University

Justin Bishop has written an extraordinary book of personal testimony, theological reflection, and technical tips to encourage and empower leaders of worship in any religious community to discover God, the omnipresent, has been online from the beginning, but people need your help to sense that presence. Bishop draws elegantly and incisively on the Fathers of the Church, his toddler son, the Bible, and the community of his own church to discover God-with-us in every moment, and in every moment to find an opportunity to share God's presence with others. The valuable technical information Bishop provides leaders of worship are grounded in the principles of gospel communication he clarifies. Bishop's confessional and theological reflections along the way proclaim that for any worship in any moment we must first return to trust in our evermore immanent God-with-us who calls us to learn anew how to reach and love one another.

—*Rev. Michael W. McCann*
Retired priest in the Episcopal Diocese of Atlanta

SENSING GOD ONLINE

Smyth & Helwys Publishing, Inc.
6316 Peake Road
Macon, Georgia 31210-3960
1-800-747-3016
©2021 by Justin Bishop
All rights reserved.

Cover photo credit: Rodion Kutsaev/Unsplash

Library of Congress Cataloging-in-Publication Data on file

SENSING GOD ONLINE

Navigating Worship in a Digital World

JUSTIN BISHOP

DEDICATION

This book is dedicated to those who do the hard work of worship—of meeting people where they are and endeavoring to lead their lives closer to God. This book is dedicated to those who craft the experience of the divine encounter week after week, seeking ways to make the presence of God a tangible reality.

ACKNOWLEDGMENTS

I am grateful for the enduring support of Heritage Fellowship in Canton, Georgia, for entrusting me with the task of leading worship and supporting my efforts in writing this book. For his faithful leadership, vision, and guidance, I am grateful for my supervisor and mentor, Dr. Rob Nash, and his encouragement throughout my doctoral work at the McAfee School of Theology. McAfee professors Dr. Karen Massey, Dr. David G. Garber, Jr., and Dr. Graham Walker guided my work and pointed me in the direction of valuable resources. My friend and mentor Michael McCann has walked with me throughout my academic and professional journey, and his feedback on my ideas has given me valuable guidance. My colleagues Kep Pate and Dr. Shaun King offered firsthand accounts of their journeys navigating digital worship during the pandemic. Many thanks to Cyndi Parr for reading the manuscript and offering insight. Dr. Jim Walls has offered guidance and leadership as both my ministry and life coach. I am forever grateful to my parents for instilling in me a life of faith.

Most of all, thanks to my wife and family for supporting these efforts through the random times when inspiration would strike and I would need to hide away and write for half an hour. Your love and support sustained me through it all.

CONTENTS

A NOTE FROM THE AUTHOR

The church's worship traditions are a double-edged sword in a digital culture. What worked then still works now, but there is an increasing number of reasons that people can't or won't come to church on Sunday. Why not take church to them?

What once cost a fortune and needed a small army to run can now be accomplished by one teenager with a smartphone. The world and its culture have changed dramatically since the advent of pocket-sized connectivity, yet many churches have ignored this potential point of connection with the world for a number of valid reasons: not enough time, money, know-how, return on investment—or simply fear that, if given the option to stay at home, people might choose never to set foot in the building again.

Connecting with the congregation both in person and online is not as simple as starting a Facebook page and watching the masses flood into your church. But it is as meaningful as having a homebound member send you a handwritten note about how much they enjoyed your sermon after being able to "tune in" for the first time in years because of technology.

We are the body of Christ. Wherever we go, there is the presence of God. It's time for us to go online.

If you're reading this, you probably lived through the COVID-19 pandemic of 2020 and beyond as churches everywhere struggled with how to continue *being church* when they couldn't *be in* church—when meeting in the building was not possible due to safety concerns. This meant a dramatic paradigm shift for countless churches, with Thom Rainer estimating "that more than 100,000 churches that had never had an internet presence beyond a website began streaming their worship services during the pandemic. And more than 250,000 congregations had never had a digital presence of any kind before the quarantine. Our numbers are broad estimates but nonetheless mind-boggling."[1]

Many turned to Facebook Live, YouTube, Zoom, and any number of other tools with which they might have already been familiar. What many discovered was that it's easier than they thought to survive in the online world. This book is designed to help you move from surviving to thriving.

The initial surge of online services and the accompanying enthusiasm were overshadowed by the pandemic fatigue felt universally by both creators and consumers of worship media. Many churches returned to in-person worship relatively quickly after the first lockdown, but ongoing health concerns meant that not everyone returned, even among those who desired to do so. The new model became *hybrid worship*, a mix between in person and online. What started as a necessity to continue to reach a community at home has now become the expectation for the twenty-first-century church. The question of how to provide for those who choose to or must stay at home creates an additional burden for an already overworked church staff. Results have been a mixed bag, and many fell into the trap of doing neither form of worship well—in person or online. It's difficult to accomplish these two things at once, especially for a small church with minimal staff and resources. This book is designed to help you navigate the challenges and maintain a healthy balance for a long-term, permanent hybrid model.

Why continue online worship indefinitely? Think about the advantages for both newcomers and standby members:

• Potential members can "attend" your worship services before they even step in the door, so they can get a feel for who you are before they ever arrive. Those who have recently relocated to your area or who are "church shopping" will have an easier time finding your church and discovering who you are as a community.
• Families on vacation can stay connected and follow church life no matter how busy their weekend lives become. Joining the traveling sports team (baseball, basketball, equestrian, cheerleading—you name it!) will no longer be a choice that results in complete isolation from their church community. And extended, out-of-state business trips will no longer come with an added price tag of not knowing what's going on at church or a neglected spiritual life.
• Sick members will feel less obligated to attend in-person services knowing that they can tune in at home. Cold and flu season might mean more empty seats in the sanctuary, but now members can worship while keeping their community healthy.

- Homebound members can reconnect with the community with a renewed sense of being in and belonging to church life.
- Hospitalized members might get to hear the prayers voiced on their behalf during the worship service.
- We live in a fast-paced, over-committed society where sabbath time is rare. Those (especially introverts) who just need some downtime and rest over the weekend can watch the sermon from their easy chair and recharge their batteries while still staying connected.
- Your message will be available at any time for those in need. The parent who missed half the sermon taking their child to the bathroom, the night-shift worker who fell asleep, the person whose mind wandered—all of these can tune in later.
- Those who missed a particular Sunday for whatever reason now have a chance to worship on their own time and terms.

There's also the theological reflection that comes with asking the question of how to worship online. What exactly are we doing each week? How much of it is necessary? What is the role of the worshiper in the room or online? Is there a difference? The televangelist has been around (and often despised!) for decades. It's time for authentic worship to be facilitated confidently online by local ministers who are already good at what they do.

For example online services, video tutorials on technical advice, and a comprehensive list of recommended gear, visit SensingGodOnline.com.

Why "Sensing" God Online?

The purpose of worship is to enable those who are present to *sense* the presence of God for both *revelation* and *response*. In other words, the goal is for them to *hear* a word from God and discover a path to *do* something about it. The senses are our primary means of perceiving the world, and they provide the best concrete metaphors with which to describe the abstract *nudging* of the Holy Spirit:[2]

As Christians, we long for more meaning in the midst of our busy lives. We often feel like we are missing out on something but can't put our fingers on what it is. We go to church and try to achieve a sense of deeper spirituality, but as soon as we walk out the doors, that feeling leaves, and we're back to square one. We know what we think about God and what we ought to believe, but what we believe so rarely escapes into the real world and sets its rhythms in our lives. We are *hungry* for more, *thirsty* to drink of deeper waters, seeking to *touch* the face of the divine. We want to *see* God's presence at work in every corner our lives. Isn't it amazing how so many of the ways that we talk about our growth in faith are *sensory metaphors*?[3]

Sensory language is our best means of making the divine tangible, perceptible. In an age when worshipers are already swimming in the waters of digital media, the worship leader must learn to navigate these waters with skill in order to avoid drowning and to ultimately reach our desired destination: the authentic worship of God.

INTRODUCTION

Since the Reformation, much of Protestant worship has been limited to the passive act of listening to some music and a sermon, and with the advent of online worship necessitated by the novel coronavirus pandemic of 2020, worship runs the risk of becoming even more passive—just another video to consume. However, whether online or in person, there are creative ways a worship leader might draw the "audience" into a more participatory role, stemming from both contemporary trends and historic traditions that make the experience of worship more engaging, appealing to all five senses, and requiring active participation. When I first stepped into the fifteenth-century Anglican chapel at Magdalen College, Oxford, I not only had a sense of traveling back in time but also had the experience of entering an atmosphere of worship long before the worship service began. The smell of incense lingered in the air, giving the light a smoky pathway to trace and creating a presence that one could almost taste. The sight of the stained-glass windows and ornate carvings told visual stories of biblical figures. I saw several people before me bow and cross themselves as they entered, and so I did the same, engaging the sense of touch. Echoes from footsteps lingered long after the footsteps themselves had ceased. And then the service started. The organ music didn't just emanate from a corner of the room—it filled the entire sanctuary, deep bass notes that I could feel reverberating throughout my body. The procession was colorful, with holy vestments glimmering in the light filtering through the icons. The priest didn't just speak; he called for a response, and the congregation followed suit. The smell of incense grew stronger. The sermon was short and decentralized but precise and to the point. We walked up front and made a cross with our hands, receiving the wafer, the strong taste of the wine hard to ignore. I had become an active, engaged participant in worship. It was an immersive, sensory experience that "broke the script" and brought worship to life. Can this translate to the digital world? Is it possible to sense and experience the presence of God through online worship?

The tendency for the modern pastor is to *transliterate* worship—that is, to do the same things online that they've been doing for in-person worship, but those elements usually don't translate. This book explores ways to facilitate the authentic divine encounter through digital means. Pastors and church staff are often left navigating uncharted waters when they venture out of the church building and into the online realm, and this book offers insights to navigate this new reality and stay afloat by reaching a broader audience more effectively.

Part 1 (the first six chapters) provides a historical and biblical assessment of what worship is and how it works, making a case for this new online iteration of a millennia-old tradition. Part 2 offers practical guidance on acquiring skills to implement the technology available to the twenty-first-century church looking to build an online presence and facilitate an authentic divine encounter through digital media. Feel free to skip around to the chapters that meet your immediate needs.

The 2020 pandemic created conditions where meeting in a sacred space was not possible, and video services were produced out of necessity. Even before the pandemic, though, not every worship service led to an authentic sacred encounter with God. A variety of distracting factors influence this outcome: loud or unexpected noises, faulty technical equipment, personal stylistic preferences, personal dilemmas or disputes, poor public speaking, wrong notes in the music, disjointed elements of the service, etc. The list of distractions only grows when the worshiper is watching a video at home instead of sitting in the sanctuary. Some of these are outside the control of the worship leader. However, if the worship planner intentionally selects cohesive elements that engage the participant at a variety of sensory levels, then the experience takes on the aura of an immersive ritual journey, minimizing the effects of the distractions listed above and ushering the participant into the mysterious presence of God. For this to happen, participants must encounter elements that focus their attention on the narrative unfolding in the worship event. In other words, every element must focus on a unified theme.

The problem is that participants enter worship with various misunderstandings and preconceived expectations about their role in worship and the overall purpose of worship. Even the word "participant" is problematic as a description of the role. Some people view the worship event as a pastime where they will "get something out of it." For these individuals, worship has become an arena for a passive audience rather than a stage[4] for active participants. If the worship planner wants to overcome the obstacle of these expectations and misunderstandings, the worship encounter with God must be carefully crafted to immerse and actively engage the worshiper in the experience. Based on my experiences as a study-abroad college student attending an Anglican sung Eucharist for the first time at Oxford and then as a pastor processing feedback on a variety of worship experiences, sensory experiences can enhance worship and provide more opportunities to take an active role in worship. Some of these practices have a long history in Roman Catholic, Orthodox, and Anglican traditions. The problem is how to reclaim all five senses for a congregation whose tradition historically has engaged only the sense of sound with music and spoken word. If worshipers at your church were encouraged to take a more active role in sensory worship, what effect would this have on their experience and perception of worship? And how do we take these experiences and *translate* them to an online environment (versus merely *transliterating* them, i.e., simply filming the same things you've always done in the building)? *We must move beyond merely transliterating in-person worship to virtual worship and instead learn how to translate from one medium to the other.*

Let's start by defining worship. Worship is the sacred encounter with God, including ritual, revelation, response to God, relationship building, and rehearsal of "love, justice, and peace in preparation for life in the world."[5] Traditions and practices have varied throughout church history, many of which the Protestant Reformation abandoned. A sensory experience is a worship element that engages one or more of the five senses (sight, sound, touch, taste, smell).

In the worship context, examples would include—

sight	visual images such as banners, videos, or pictures displayed on a screen or on paper, or lighting;
sound	spoken word, music, recorded sounds, etc.;
touch	an object lesson (something to hold), kneeling, performing the sign of the cross, holding hands during a prayer or benediction, crossing hands to receive the bread during Communion;
taste	tasting the bread and juice or wine during Communion, eating any other symbolic food;
smell	incense or scented candles, fresh bread being baked in the building, real greenery.

Experiential worship employs multiple sensory elements to enhance the experience, marking a sharper contrast between worship and daily life and deepening the connection to and experience of God in a corporate gathering.

Some traditions have held on to a few worship practices that require active participation (crossing oneself, responding to the liturgy, kneeling for prayer, walking up front for Communion, etc.), but many Protestant traditions are content with just *going* to church. Once you go into the building, you've met your requirement for active participation—to just show up! There's got to be something more, right? Being invited to stand and sing along with the music is a start, but it's possible for people to be swimming in the water of a passive role in worship where the only requirements are to watch and listen. In a digital era where the passive consumption of visual media creates a culture of disengaged worshipers, the worship leader can cultivate more active participation through the incorporation of sensory experiences both in the room and on the screen. The ideas contained in this book can transform your worship practices in the room, but the primary goal is to translate what you do in the room into a format that more actively engages worshipers who join you online. The unifying thread is worship engagement through sensory experiences. We speak of having been "moved" by a service, and this book seeks to intentionally create more opportunities to sense the presence and movement of God's Spirit in an online format.

Part one makes a case for the theological, biblical, and historical evolution of worship practices and seeks to trace the role of sensory experiences throughout various contexts in history. The main idea is that worship has always been about more than just watching and listening to music and a sermon. Part two reimagines what worship can look like in an online platform and offers ideas for making the experience more engaging through sensory elements. Navigating this digital world requires a skill set with which many worship architects have familiarity only in passing. We are used to consuming digital media, but the creation of an engaging worship experience online presents a peculiar challenge. Doing what you've always done and simply placing a camera in front of it doesn't necessarily translate well on the other side of the screen, and the experience is enhanced the more senses you can involve in the act of worship.

PART 1

Theological Foundations of Worship

CHAPTER 1

WORSHIP IS A VERB

The Water We're Swimming In

There's a story that goes something like this: Two fish are swimming upstream, chatting away, when an older fish swimming the opposite direction nods and says, "How's the water?" Perplexed, one of the two younger fish leans toward the other and says, "What's water?"

Most ministers and church leaders have been swimming in church life their entire lives, and they can't see the water they're swimming in. We spend so much time focused on the word *church* (getting people to come to church, maintaining the appearance of the church, assessing the financial and spiritual health of the church) that we forget what the *church* is for—worship!

Now that there's a precedent for digital media and "online church," you can't do what you've always done and expect the same results. You wouldn't plant watermelon in the desert or release a tropical fish into a mountain stream. The environment would be all wrong. The truth is, our "consumer-minded" churchgoers have been swimming in the waters of digital media for years, and the church is only now being forced to catch up because of the pandemic and its aftermath. This chapter explores the effects of cultural trends in technology that are challenging our understanding of worship and the role our participants play in it. Is just showing up enough? Or can more active participation become the expectation?

Transliterating Worship

In transitioning to digital worship, our instinct is to do the same thing we've always done but simply figure out how to do it online. The problem is that it doesn't translate, much like how *transliterating*[6] a word from ancient Greek or Hebrew to English letters is often just as meaningless as the original if the reader is unfamiliar with the language. You might be able to better pronounce the word *barak* if you see it as the transliteration of *barak* instead of בְּרָךְ, but you still won't know that it means "blessing" without a *translation*. We must learn to translate worship for an online experience if we are going to communicate our message effectively in the twenty-first century.

If the COVID-19 pandemic taught us anything about church, it taught us that there is much more involved in "going to church" than just listening to a sermon. There is a social and community aspect that fills a human need as much if not more than the spiritual aspect of singing hymns, reading Scripture, and hearing a preacher's message.

If we're honest with ourselves, we'll admit that much of what happens during the actual worship service could be both better and more efficient, but we've never noticed or given it much thought since people will sit through an hour-long (or more) service because the entire experience is meaningful to them. You might think that a few unenjoyable moments might ruin an experience, but it seems that the brain has learned to filter those out. We can have an experience where 90 percent is unenjoyable or even frustrating and miserable (like waiting in line for rides at Disney), but people will remember the key powerful and meaningful moments because "in recalling an experience, we ignore most of what happened and focus instead on a few particular moments."[7]

Even if they were miserable *most* of the time, if they found joy in one moment, then that brief experience will take over in their memory. They will rate the whole experience a nine out of ten when, most of the time, it was a four. In-person worship means a captive audience; even if they like only one out of four hymns and the guest preacher is boring, if their granddaughter read Scripture (or there was a single meaningful event such as a baptism or a lovely solo or a catchy phrase or sermon illustration), they will say it was a "great service" overall—and they will mean it.

Online worship, however, is different, and people are less likely to "tune in" for the entire hour if they lose interest. This is largely the result of years of "consuming" visual media on television. We have conditioned ourselves to take a break during the commercials or to change the channel if the pace gets too slow. For online worship, this means that when consumer worshipers have the option to click away or turn the screen off, the instinct is for worship to become just another piece of media to consume in an already oversaturated market. The truth is that if you put exactly what you've always done on the screen, few people will have the patience to engage with it authentically. There is something fundamentally different about being in a room with a body of believers versus sitting in your easy chair with a screen in front of you.

Still, it is worth it to stick a tripod in the back of the room and live-stream the whole service.[8] But you can do better, and when you engage in the process of thinking about what might work better on-screen, your in-person experience may also be transformed for the better. Do you need seven minutes for announcements? Is the fifth verse of the hymn truly worth singing? The answer might be yes to both questions, but by asking them, you've taken one step further down the path toward intentional rather than rote worship.

The simple rule of online content is "less is more." The irony of the universal availability of information is that there is too much to process at any given time, and so people's minds learn, out of necessity, to filter information. There's too much out there to pay attention to everything, so the default is to focus only on things that grab our attention. Regular social media consumers scroll through thousands of messages a day, pausing on something for only seconds before deciding to move on.

Online worship can easily become just another piece of content on which to pause briefly and then move on. Furthermore, viewers can start to mistake the role of worshiper for the role of the consumer. In the absence of a congregation, congregational singing is all but impossible, along with all the other communal aspects of being together. But this does not mean that *authentic connection* isn't possible online. It just looks different and feels different. Take, for example, your favorite fictional cinematic movie. Do you not escape reality briefly and put yourself inside the story? You are *connecting* with that story even though it is on the screen. What is the difference between that movie and an online worship service? For one thing, the movie has a story that moves the action along, and for another, it offers high-quality video and audio production. The movie takes you on a journey, and it looks and sounds great, so you connect with it.

Even without the same production budgets and resources as Hollywood, churches can follow the same three simple rules:

1. Follow a story line.
2. Make it look good.
3. Make it sound good.

Cinema and worship might have different endgames in mind, but the medium and goals are similar: to create an *authentic connection*. To make this happen, we can follow the steps outlined in the book *The Power of Moments: Why Certain Experiences Have Extraordinary Impact.*

> To create moments of connection, we can bring people together for a synchronizing moment. We can invite them to share in a purposeful struggle. The final strategy centers on connecting them to a larger sense of meaning. In many organizations, our daily obligations—the emails, the meetings, the to-do lists—can numb us to the meaning of our work. And that sense of meaning can be the difference between a great performer and a mediocre one.[9]

Whether we are being entertained or formed for spiritual transformation, it is clear that our senses play a prominent role in the process. After all, in the church where I grew up, people would say after a particularly meaningful worship service, "Great service! I *felt* the Spirit today!"

Studies show that the more senses that are involved in any given undertaking, the more of a memorable impact that experience has.[10] Therefore, the online worship architect must engage as many of these senses as possible to facilitate the worshiper's assumption of an active role in the worship of God.

Transliterated Worship	**Translated Worship**
Doing what you've always done in worship but filming it.	*Rethinking and reshaping your approach to worship to fit a screen medium.*
• Putting a camera in the back of the room with a wide angle that catches everything happening in the building.	• Using a multi-camera view with a variety of camera angles to focus attention.
	• Displaying text on the screen to indicate the order and flow of worship.
• Posting a picture of the church bulletin to social media.	• Displaying the lyrics in time with the music so that people can sing or hum along.
• Broadcasting the choir singing a hymn.	
	• Displaying the text of the Scripture reading so that worshipers can read along.
• Broadcasting someone reading Scripture.	• Displaying PowerPoint slides and images to convey key points of the sermon.
• Printing a sermon outline in the bulletin.	• Cutting to a prerecorded message outlining ways to respond while at home. ("If you'd like to learn more about our community, or if we can pray with you, give us a call at this number.")
• Giving an invitation or announcing a time of response, allowing people to come down to the front of the church.	

Let's take a closer look at what's happening in the worship event, and then we might better discover how to translate what we do to an online arena. Before we can make it look better and sound better, we have to first clarify exactly what we're doing in worship.

Worship as Dialogue: Creating Revelation and Response Online

We like to think that the act of going to church is a participatory event that requires some active role from the participant. But look at how we describe it. People don't say, "I engaged in worship of the Almighty today." Instead, they simply say, "I went to church." Yes, getting them to go is a big part of the challenge, but once they're in the building, it takes some effort to move them beyond seeing the worship event as merely a spectacle to behold. An occasional sermon series on worship is not enough to combat the "consumer" culture that lumps "going to church" into the same category as "going to a movie," "going to a sporting event," or "going to a play or concert." We tend to see all of these as events where we sit, watch, and listen to something entertaining. It's no wonder people view worship the same way.

It takes deliberate effort to create a culture of active worship instead of just a group of people who "go to church" (though the latter is a challenge in itself!). The easiest place to begin this shift in perspective is with the response. How do you describe what is happening in the last few minutes of worship? Is it an invitation? A time of response? Have you unpacked what this means for your congregation? If they grew up like I did, then the main reason for going to church was to see the "lost" get "saved." While this is certainly of primary concern, isn't there more? Isn't there something about worship that demands a response from all in attendance and not just from those who have never made a profession of faith? This concept needs unpacking and extra emphasis every Sunday if it is to reconstruct your congregation's view of worship, especially if you frequently see new families joining.

One way of describing the difference between active and passive worship is to use the words "revelation" and "response" more frequently in both spoken and written word. You could print these words as headings in your bulletin in key parts of your liturgy because they intertwine throughout the service (not just at the end!). The call to worship then becomes a call to attention, to seek recognition of how God might be speaking and offering "revelation" throughout the service. And in order for this revelation not to ring hollow, it must be followed by response. In order for this paradigm to become a part of your church's identity, it takes deliberate weekly effort and specific language cues. A sermon series or book study is a start, but it's not enough to build a lasting culture of active worshipers.

Let's take a look at a few places where "revelation" and "response" might fit into the service. My church has an "offertory hymn" followed by the "offertory." This is a perfect place to insert a label of "revelation" for the hymn and "response" for the offering (either spoken or printed in the bulletin), and it offers a way of transforming how people see what they're doing in that moment. This may not be a good place to start if there has been bickering over financial matters in your group, but it is a prime example of how you can connect the act of tithing with the ancient practice of sacrifice and the theology of worship as, literally and etymologically, the act of "conveying worth" to something—in this case to God. An older generation might give automatically because it's "the right thing to do," but others might need help in seeing their offering as an act of worship.

The next easy place for emphasizing the active worship paradigm is near the end of your service. What if you labeled your sermon as "revelation" and what happens after it as "response"? This implies something more universal than the word "invitation," which has historically been associated with inviting "the lost" to come and receive salvation. During the final song, the worship leader might invite reflection on God's calling in each person's life that day. Then the benediction can wrap up the service with a charge to "Go from this place seeking to . . ." (insert active verbs of response here).

How many attendees might never even consider the word "worship" as part of the experience? They're simply "going" to church. This is where your "language house"[11] becomes incredibly important for transforming attitudes and reshaping how churchgoers view their role in what is happening during the worship event.

The "Language House" of Worship

A picture held us captive. . . . And we could not get outside of it, for it lay in our language and language seemed to repeat it to us inexorably.
                            —Ludwig Wittgenstein, *Philosophical Investigations*

Language is the house of Being. In its home man dwells. Those who think and those who create with words are the guardians of this home.
                            —Martin Heidegger, *Letter on Humanism*[12]

"Welcome to church!"

"Come, let us prepare our hearts for worship."

Can you hear the difference in these two statements? It might seem insignificant, but these short sentences that we tag onto the end of our welcome, announcements, or calls to worship make a big difference in shaping the tone and focus for the entire service.

In his book *Missional: Joining God in the Neighborhood*, Alan Roxburgh asks how different church would be if we stopped having so many conversations about "church." He takes the reader through the challenges for the early Christians in Luke-Acts as they navigated the emerging path of following Jesus, a path in which they "were being challenged to let go of a deeply entrenched imagination and trust that God was up to something radically outside anything they had come to expect."[13]

To be a part of what God was up to in Jesus they needed a new "language house," and if we recognize that God is at work in the world apart from the limited reaches of our individual churches, then we must embrace a new language house so we can move beyond simply trying to get more people to come to church. There must be more to it than getting people in the building, so we must transform the way we talk about what we're doing and work against our instinct to focus so much on "church" alone. We need a new language house.

What is a language house? It's the way we imagine who we are and find our identity in the world. As Roxburgh explains,

> A community's imagination, its stories and practices, its history and expectations—these are created and carried by words that interpret everything. We are constructed by and live our lives in and through language; not language as we have come to understand it as a tool, as positivism or propaganda, but more like a "house of language."[14]

You may not think people take much stock in what you say, but why would they get so angry when they disagree if what you say doesn't matter to them? Words matter, and public words from a pulpit shape people's views of the world, the church, and themselves. And yes, they may not agree with everything you say, or they may "zone out" during your sermon from time to time, but if you have built your language house on a "rock," then your strong foundation shall not be shaken (Matt 16:18; Luke 4:48). Your words are far more than wind:

Language isn't like inert brick or construction timber. It is far more! It is
the house where our humanity is formed and continually made over; it
gives expression to our deepest senses of who we are, the mystery of what
it means to be human in a world that does not go on forever—where we
create and die. Language is the realm of the poet, of desire and hope, of
the search for and expression of infinity.[15]

This idea suggests that those subtle, off-script moments—when you are
speaking off the cuff to deliver announcements or just to transition between
elements—should not be discounted as insignificant. Everything you
say from the pulpit matters, and words should be chosen carefully, especially motifs or mantras that you repeat. Pay attention to these unscripted
moments. Go back and watch video of the things you say when you haven't
planned it all out, and ask yourself these questions:
• Is it necessary?
• Does it contribute to the overall theme?
• Does it draw people further into the worship moment?
If the answer is "no" to any of these questions, reconsider what you have to
say, and consider scripting these parts as well.

There are multiple perspectives from which we experience the divine.
Why does this matter? In American Protestantism in the aftermath of
the Great Awakenings and Revivalist movements, our primary "language
house" has emphasized mostly the perspective focusing on condemnation
and forgiveness.[16] This perspective is marked by an emphasis on sin and
repentance. However, theologians have more recently noted that this is
merely *a* perspective but not *the* perspective. Consequently, there is something missing for people who inhabit or highly value a different perspective.
Therefore, we have work to do to expand our language house, reach those
with different perspectives, and ultimately fulfill our multifaceted calling as
builders of the Kingdom of God. To acknowledge the breadth and diversity
of our calling is to embrace a greater variety of themes for worship, opening
the door for God's revelation on topics other than sin and forgiveness. In
other words, evangelism might be *the* most important task of the church,
but discipleship should be a close second. If your language house is only
about "bringing them into the faith," look for ways to "move them further
along in the faith." After all, with stronger disciples, it follows that your
church's outreach will increase, whether those impacted people join your
church or not. At least you will have made a difference in their lives and in
the world.

When it comes to the specific language house of worship, we as leaders must move from a focus on "isn't it good to be in church?" to "come, let us worship the Lord together." One highlights simply *being* there in the church while the other implies active participation from everyone present. A change in that phrase alone, during the welcome or call to worship, can begin to shift the perspectives of those present. Are they just *there*, or are they actively engaged? Did they just come to *church*? Or did they come to *worship*? There's an important difference between *church* as a noun and *worship* as a verb, and when we convey that difference, we have established a firm foundation for your new language house.

The Worship Architect: Becoming a Poet

People already inhabit God's story, but congregations may need help to see it. Putting a worship service together is more than selecting the right hymns and following the prescribed liturgy of your context.[17] The word *liturgy* itself comes from "the Greek *leitourgía*, composed from words for work (*érgon*) and people (*laós*). In ancient Greece, a liturgy was a public work performed for the benefit of the city or state." [18] So today one might interpret the meaning literally as "the work for the people" or "any work done for the common welfare." Translated into a more recent context, "church leaders and theologians have stressed this derivation of 'liturgy,' since it points to worship as the work of the whole people of God, and not just the clergy."[19] The point here is that we need to emphasize the "service" part of the term "worship service" and help worshipers see their deeds and the way they live their lives when they leave the church are all part of a bigger picture of worship as an act in which to participate rather than a spectacle to observe. To acknowledge this reality, the people need help understanding their role in the unfolding drama—their part in the story. Hence the role of the worship leader is to facilitate this paradigm shift from seeing worship as a story to behold versus a story which one already inhabits and plays a vital role. In other words, worship is the unfolding of God's story so that those present might recognize their part to play in order to move that story further along. As a worship leader, when you seek and follow the nudging of the Spirit in your worship planning, a particular part of God's story begins to emerge, along with an accompanying theme. As the architect of this story, you are building a path for a transformative journey, creating an avenue for people to sense the presence of God in their everyday comings and goings. You are a poet in the original sense of the word.

The Greek (*poiein*) roots of poem and poetry have to do with "making" or "crafting" something. So think of yourself as a "worship craftsman," and realize that what you are doing is an art form with a goal: to usher your attendees into the presence of God so they might walk away with a renewed vision of their calling and purpose in this life. You're creating a space for both revelation *and* response. And just as an author leads a reader to a theme, a revelation about life and living, so too must you craft your worship events with careful attention to the exposition, the rising action, the climax, the falling action, and the resolution. Subtle language cues can shepherd your flock along this journey every Sunday.

People come to church for all kinds of reasons, but a big part of their desire to congregate is for help navigating life's challenges. They want someone to pray beside their hospital bed, to show up late at night when tragedy strikes, to offer light in life's darkness. Life is filled with crises. How does the church meet people's needs? What does worship have to do with any of this? It all starts with story.

The Babylonian exile began after God's temple was destroyed, along with most of the city of Jerusalem. The survivors were carted off to Babylon, where they faced the existential crisis of how to worship with their "church" (the temple) and how to maintain their identity while living among the foreign culture of their invaders. The psalmist sums it up with the question, "How could we sing the LORD's song in a foreign land?" (Ps 137:4). How did they hold themselves together? They reformed their worship practices, incorporating story as a way to keep their identity and their faith alive.[20] Small groups gathered whenever possible, and Scripture reading became common, particularly from the books of the Torah (the first five books of the Bible, the "Books of Moses"). These exiles held on to who they were by telling their story, God's story. We could do well to follow their example.

The people of God living in exile edited their story to fit their context, and biblical scholars attribute numerous "Psalms of Lament" and other expressions of grief and theological speculation to this period of questioning why bad things were happening to good people. This is proof that, while God's story has the power to reach any generation, its successful communication depends largely on how you craft the story to fit your context. We must become poets of God's story, and our parchment is the video screen in this digital age.

What is a poet? Roxburgh describes this person as "one who listens to the stories that lie beneath the stories people tell and gives voice to the music beneath their words. The poet is the one who, in such listening, offers ways in which people can connect this music to a larger movement, to a bigger story."[21] Worship is our avenue for telling God's story and for holding together the identity of God's people in the midst of crisis.

To immerse worshipers in that story, the worship leader might subtly insert motifs throughout the service: song introductions, calls to worship, prayers, dramatic readings, introductions to Scripture reading. Maybe you've connected the dots in your mind as to why you've made certain choices, but your worshipers need little hints to help them see the big picture. However, it is equally important to avoid sounding pedantic or over-explaining your selections. Using words like "I chose this hymn because it says in verse 3 that . . ." can have the opposite of your desired effect, landing abrasively on your worshipers' ears and breaking the flow of worship to insert a "Look what I did!" moment that's more about you than the song or the storied theme of worship.

There is an art to striking a balance with how many extra words are built into the service. I've heard of pastors who tell their worship leaders, "You leave the preaching to me!" It's easy to say too much about something that is your passion. I once led worship for a summer youth camp. Each week, adult chaperones would fill out feedback cards, and I would have to read their comments. In one week, I would get comments like "I just loved the worship leader's introductions to the songs! They made the music come alive in new ways to me." Another comment might read, "I wish the worship leader would just sing instead of talking so much." These people sat through the same worship experiences with different perspectives. Keep in mind that you will find these varied perspectives for every element of worship, no matter what choices you make: "What a fresh new song!" versus "Why did we end with a song that nobody knew?" It doesn't mean you shouldn't try new things or insert extra words into the flow of worship. Just try to strike a balance and choose wisely!

The sacred encounter with God in worship remains a mystery. We sense when it happens, even if it is hard to put into words what we've just experienced. Often the experience of the ineffable surfaces in conversation only in the inadequate terms we have at our disposal, such as "That was great!" or "Wonderful service!" or "Today was such a blessing," uttered in benignly emphatic tones on the way out the door. We're not sure exactly what to talk about, yet those are the services after which everyone *is* talking, the participants remarking on the experience even if they can't articulate precisely what made the difference. Sometimes all the pieces fall into place, making the story come alive, creating liminal space for an authentic sacred encounter. But not every Sunday worship service succeeds in creating this experience. So what makes the difference, and is it possible to facilitate the creation of a sacred space through a video while the worshiper sits at home? I suspect that engagement and cohesiveness enhance the worship experience, whether online or in person. When all the senses are drawn into the act of worship and when all the pieces of worship fit together to tell a unified story, that's when the experience of God becomes most palpable. And if participants adopt a more active view of their role in worship, perhaps they will also adopt a more active view of their role as Christians in the world.

My Ministerial Context: A Small Suburban Church

Over the years, the world has seen a myriad of arrangements of worship elements to usher participants into the presence of God. Every church has a liturgy, even if not every church would be comfortable with the word "liturgical." The order of service was particularly important to the founders of Heritage Fellowship in Canton, Georgia, when they chose to break away from the Southern Baptist Convention in the late 1990s, citing, among other things, a "lack of integrity" in worship as one reason for the split. I have heard numerous members speak about the pitfalls of the "emotional manipulation" they see employed in some worship practices ranging from fear-based, "fire-and-brimstone" sermons to loud rock music "putting on a show" for mere entertainment value. The church wanted to avoid those trending extremes and get back to the basics of a traditional worship service, going so far as to choose the word "heritage" as part of their name.

This does not mean they oppose innovation. Renovations made early in 2019 included the controversial addition of televisions at the front of the sanctuary. This change to the worship space could have divided the congregation, but there has been near unanimous support for the addition of visual elements to enhance worship, an indication of a concerted effort to keep worship practices vibrant at every level, including the sermon. In my five years as worship pastor there, I've watched as a change in senior pastoral leadership led to a transition from a sermon-series approach to a lectionary-based system of worship planning. As I've stood in the back of the church shaking hands with our average crowd of roughly sixty retirees and a handful of younger members, comments range from "Have a great week" to "Nice music!" to "Wow, what a great service today!" In my doctor of ministry (DMin) project, I sought to determine if the inclusion of more sensory elements in digital worship would result in worshipers walking away with the "Wow, what a great service!" feeling.

An Example of Digital Worship

What does digital worship with a sensory experience look like? During my doctoral project in Holy Week of 2021, the service that generated the most "Wow!" comments was the Good Friday Tenebrae/Stations of the Cross service.[22] My script was simple, beginning with a few words of explanation:

> "A Service of Tenebrae [or "Shadows"]" is based on a twelfth-century late night/early morning service and is an extended meditation on the passion of Christ. Let our words tonight draw you further into the story. For this experience to work best, find a comfortable place in a completely dark room in your home, turning off all other lights except for seven candles if you have them available. You may wish to have a flashlight, for the experience should end in total darkness. Pause the video now and make preparations with a dark room and seven lit candles.
>
> As each piece of the story is finished, extinguish a candle, and allow yourself to be drawn further down the path on this journey with Jesus to the cross.

The sensory element was the candles and darkness, facilitating the immersion in the story of Jesus' final journey to the cross, marking each step on the journey by physically extinguishing a candle which immersed the worshiper deeper into darkness. Between each step, the story was read aloud from Scripture, chiefly John 18. This same service would work in person in a darkened sanctuary, but in a digital format, I was able to synchronize the words being read with a visual representation of the story from *The Gospel of John* by the Jesus Film Project after obtaining permission for use of the film in our video services. This visual experience, coupled with accompanying song "What Wondrous Love" led to many comments from worshipers on how meaningful the service was for them and how it drew them further into the story, helping them see parts of it they had never before considered. They had a simple task to *do*—to extinguish the candles, but it gave them an active role to keep and focus their attention. The entire service ended with a challenge: What does this wondrous love require of us?[23]

How might you create something like this in your context? The following chapters are designed to help you navigate worship in our digital world and empower you to create worship experiences which fit your context. Begin by reminding yourself that worship is something we want our churches to *do* rather than something we *attend* or *observe*. Consider ways that you might encourage more active participation in worship whether online or in person.

What do we *do* when we worship? We come together on Sunday in a gathering that "includes prayer, the reading of Scripture, preaching, singing, and a blessing and charge to live faithfully in the world."[24] How might you further engage the people there so that they might become *participants* rather than *attendees*?

CHAPTER 2

THE SHIFT

The Pandemic of 2020

In March 2020, the COVID-19 pandemic struck America with widespread school, business, and church closures and state lockdowns. Worship gatherings at churches were especially dangerous due to the prolonged proximity of groups gathering indoors, and congregations that continued to meet risked their services becoming "super-spreader" events.[25] As a result, many churches (my church Heritage Fellowship included) made "the shift" and transitioned to online worship to maintain the safety of their members. Various sources indicate that the initial switch to online worship occurred quickly for most churches, many of whom had never before attempted such a feat. Recent technologies such as Facebook Live enabled ministers to continue to reach their congregations with only a smartphone as their broadcasting equipment. During the early months of the pandemic, many churches reported a much greater attendance online than they had experienced in person, and I can confirm that Heritage Fellowship went from reaching an average of one hundred people in person each month to reaching an average of over one thousand for several months throughout the early part of the pandemic. This does not mean that high number of people watched every worship service all the way through, but the analytics on Facebook indicate that each month more than a thousand people saw a post that we created. These are the positive sides of switching to online worship.

On the other hand, online worship comes with a host of potential problems. The biggest problem is the possibility for distractions. For Heritage, our attempts at livestreaming were hindered by internet connectivity. If some worshipers tuned in live, the video would pause to buffer every few minutes, making it difficult to concentrate or focus on the message. And even if this problem was overcome by prerecording the service and publishing it later, there remained the potential distractions for someone trying to worship at home. We are inundated with media of all types, and our minds wander. We pause the worship service and tend to a chore or answer the phone, or we tune in to another internet post or television channel.

Perhaps the greatest pitfall of worship leaders treading into the uncharted digital arena is the temptation to practice "ministry translit-eration by simply changing to digital platforms and presuming that the methodology that was somewhat effective in face-to-face context would be equally or even more effective digitally."[26] The assumption here is that worship leadership can continue to do what it has always done with the only difference being that there is now a camera pointed at the pulpit. This *transliteration* of worship leaves a lot to be desired, much as a Greek or Hebrew word transliterated into English is hardly capable of conveying the same meaning that a *translation* might provide. The "effectiveness" of worship is difficult to discern on any given Sunday, but the metrics of the traditional counts of "nickels and noses" is at least a starting point. The second greatest pitfall (at least on par with the first) is that adapting to a "Worship on Demand model" can breed a kind of "worship consumerism" even as it offers the convenience of tuning in whenever *you* like, creating at best "fragmented engagement within the community of faith."[27] It inadver-tently puts the individual worshiper (and their wants, needs, desires) above the community.

At the beginning of the pandemic, the shift to online worship happened quickly, and, desperate for something "normal," worshipers "attending" online held strong. However, for churches that failed to adapt to this new reality and "consider new forms and methodologies of teaching, preaching, and pastoral care," both "attendance and engagement declined, leading to disappointment and discouragement."[28] It is safe to say that many churches will never be the same after the pandemic. What remains to be seen is how online worship will take new shape as it now has an exponential increase of both creators and explorers.

In an interview with Kep Pate, a friend and fellow youth minister who effectively adapted to virtual youth ministry,[29] I asked about his church's journey in the suburbs of Raleigh, North Carolina, which closely parallels my own church's journey on the outskirts of Metro Atlanta. He identified the pandemic journey into digital ministry as having three phases roughly three months apart:

1. The Gimmick. At first, "online church" was something new and different. We all thought it would be over quickly, in just a few weeks, and then we'd be back to normal. During this time, people loved doing simple, easy-to-plan events, and they participated with great enthusiasm. For my church, people would quickly and gladly volunteer to submit photos of flowers for Easter or another themed topic for our video worship. For Kep Pate's church, his youth group was able to easily plan virtual "watch party" movie nights, Instagram photo post challenges, and other ideas with full engagement.

2. Overcommitment. As the pandemic wore on, without an end in sight, both his church and my church settled into a pattern of oversaturating the digital realm, filling every possible moment with online devotions, Bible studies, reflections, photo challenges, etc. Even though the content was better (more thoughtfully planned and executed), the entire enterprise seemed deflated as the novelty wore off. For me, a devotional video post that would have quickly generated thirty views (or even as high as 200 or 300 if people shared it!) was now struggling to get three total views, one of which was me to preview it and make sure it worked.

3. New Normal = Authentic Connection. When it became clear that pandemic fatigue was taking its toll on both the creators' creativity and the viewers' enthusiasm, both his church and mine settled into a more modest, sustainable pattern, still with fewer participants than at first but with more than the participants in the middle phase. His church held once-a-week Sunday school/community time on Zoom (an application that inadvertently kills small talk but offers at least a chance for everyone to speak and participate if they are willing to learn and use the technology). I held a midweek devotional Zoom call during which even those in assisted living could call in to both listen and chat. What began as a one-size-fits-all approach to social media posting morphed into a renewed emphasis on small community groups or one-on-one contacts when we periodically touched base with our congregants. The emphasis shifted from digital flare to actual moments of connection, perhaps because that is what seemed to be missed the most in the isolation of pandemic life.

Through all of this, at my church, online worship "attendance" remained steady. There were a handful of people who never watched a single video, but most made an effort to create a space to "worship" at home even when they couldn't "go to church."

The New Normal

I pray that by the time you read this, the pandemic is long behind us and society has emerged from the ashes with a renewed sense of identity that hasn't just "gone back to the way it was" but has upgraded to a new and better version of its old self. But there will be a long period of reconstruction, and we will wrestle with this question for some time: what lessons from the forced journey into "digital worship" will carry over into the "new normal"?

Here's one way to answer that question:

> So much of my energy pre-pandemic was about cheap connection points and means of communicating information. I would use social media posts simply as a means to get attention and tell people when to sign up and show up to events. It was exhausting because I was constantly trying to come up with a gimmick to get better photos for Instagram, thinking that this would translate into more engagement at those events. We could create a lot of noise with that, but we never found the fruit until authentic conversation started happening. Before it was mostly me just throwing information out there, but once I started direct communication using one-on-one phone calls, text messages, and handwritten notes, I began to sense that we were moving from "noise" to "conversation"—to authentic relationship and community. We tried gimmicks and that lasted three months . . . we tried oversaturating the market . . . when the engagement stopped, it got back to just authentic community. That's what we had before, but now we had discovered how to use technology in order to achieve it. We can easily get distracted by the bright lights and smoke screens, and it's easy to fall into a pattern where, when one gimmick stops working, we just move on to the next in order to "just get kids to come to church." But to authentically engage in a real conversation with someone—that's no gimmick, and it's something that will carry over into post-pandemic life. I might never have reached out using technology before, but now I believe it will become the norm, with community-shaping power.[30]

Community in Worship

There is something sacred about space, whether attendees are conscious of it or not. And from the appearance of the building to the smiles on the faces of greeters as you enter the building, a welcoming community creates an atmosphere of freedom to belong. People were already attending less frequently (One study found a 3% decrease in weekly church attendance from 2007 to 2014.[31]), so after the pandemic, now that you've proven to yourself that a text or phone call isn't so daunting as it was before, it should be easier to maintain a community connection with someone that makes them feel more at home regardless of where they might be worshiping. If anything, the pandemic taught us that, even with all the great preachers suddenly available on demand 24/7 on the internet, most people will choose to listen to their own community with whom they have a personal connection, even if the "production value" might be lower. That sense of safety and belonging creates vulnerability and openness to be shaped and formed, allowing worship to become an occasion when people can feel "at home" in the presence of God, even if they don't have the language to articulate why they feel what they feel. And whether they are an overcommitted businesswoman getting pastoral care via email or a ninety-year-old widow in an assisted-living facility, digital media enables you to connect with them, bringing the presence of God to them by creating that sense of belonging.

Reflection: Teaching Them How to See

We cannot attain *the presence of God because we're* already in *the presence of God. What's absent is awareness. Little do we realize that God's love is maintaining us in existence with every breath we take. As we take another, it means that God is choosing us now and now and now. We have nothing to attain or even learn. We do, however, need to unlearn some things. To become aware of God's loving presence in our lives, we have to accept that human culture is in a mass hypnotic trance. We're sleep-walkers. All great religious teachers have recognized that we human beings do not naturally see; we have to be taught how to see.*

—Richard Rohr[32]

My thoughts were far away: all the things I had to do, all the questions about what was going to happen next, decisions to make, tasks to accomplish, bills to pay. Even though I was standing right next to him, I was miles away in my mind. I don't know how many times he said it before I finally heard it, but suddenly his voice broke through: "Daddy! *Sand!*" My toddler had noticed what I had missed: a patch of sand just large enough to play in beside our pond. And I was standing in it, unaware not only of its existence but also of its potential. Suddenly I became aware that if anything was going to happen, I had to get out of the way. So I stepped aside, but that wasn't enough: "Daddy! *Play!*" And so I did. We both got dirty and giggled, and I forgot whatever it was I had been worried about.

I'm not sure I understand it, but looking back, I believe it was God speaking through my son's voice that day. It was just a moment. But how many moments do we miss while worrying about moments that haven't even happened yet—not to mention those that have already happened and can't be changed?

The truth is, I believe that God is always calling us out of our own mind traps. We just learn to tune God out. Maybe it's a sunset, a song on the radio, a friend's call that we don't have time to take, or the sound of a songbird performing for no reason at all. Richard Rohr reminds us that "we are already in the presence of God. What's absent is awareness."

We must learn to awaken to the voice of God in the everyday, ordinary ways of life. We must cultivate awareness. We must practice the presence of God. This sentiment is echoed throughout Scripture, especially in Psalm 139 (NRSV):

> O LORD, you have searched me and known me.
> You know when I sit down and when I rise up;
>   you discern my thoughts from far away.
> You search out my path and my lying down,
>   and are acquainted with all my ways.
> Even before a word is on my tongue,
>   O LORD, you know it completely.
> You hem me in, behind and before,
>   and lay your hand upon me.
> Such knowledge is too wonderful for me;
>   it is so high that I cannot attain it.
> Where can I go from your spirit?
>   Or where can I flee from your presence?

We spend so much time asking questions when maybe, just maybe, we are the answer. Why can't we hear God? Maybe we're standing in the way and need to step aside. There's room in the sandbox if we learn to play together.

Good worship should cause us to step out of the way, to break free momentarily from the obsessions of self that consistently plague us. Good worship connects us to something larger than ourselves and reminds us, in the presence of God, to aim and direct our lives to God's purposes. God's presence is only as "real" as it can be perceived.

Regardless of the atmosphere in which one is attending worship, the primary task of the worship leader is to "enflesh and serve the *logos*, and true liturgy celebrates nothing but the active presence of the Three in One."[33] Whether a worshiper is sitting in an enormous Gothic cathedral in a large city, a tiny parish church in a rural village, or in their easy chair at home, the primary task of the worship leader is to usher the worshiper into an awareness of the presence of God where divine connection and personal transformation become possible. In a bygone era, stained-glass windows, incense, and elaborate rituals were enough to accomplish this task. In our modern era, many have flocked to dark concert venues with professional rock-and-roll musicians to achieve this. But in an age of a pandemic, many were left to recreate a sacred space in their homes by watching a screen. Christ may be revealed in all of these, but what do they have in common? It has everything to do with experience: "Christ is revealed when worshipers are drawn into the Word by preachers who know how to create a realm of virtual experience."[34] Experiences of the presence of God are as varied as the people who seek such an encounter, but one mark of a worship service that successfully creates this atmosphere is the comments by worshipers on the way out the door about how the service "spoke to me." The worship leadership must therefore maintain uniformity in theme and message in order to guard the service from all distractions.

DISTRACTIONS

I once taught a middle school course on technical theater, and my first lesson was simple: "The goal of the person running sound is to disappear." I could say the same for those who are running worship. We've all been in a room where the sound system erupts in screeching feedback, and the first thing everyone does is turn around and glance at the sound booth. That moment takes everyone out of the sacred space and into disruption and annoyance. The sound technician has done the best job when no one even thinks about the presence of the sound technician. I could say the same for the worship architect. Though less dramatic, a worship leader of any kind rambling or speaking off topic provides an easy opportunity for minds to wander.

While it might be impossible to eliminate all distractions, it is possible to control what language the worship leadership uses, the songs that are sung—in short, everything the people are seeing and hearing (and if Communion is involved, smelling and tasting)—and one might even direct the worshiper to touch something (place a hand over their heart, etc.). This unity creates a space in which every part plays a role in a larger undertaking—the creation of the "virtual experience." A good story can take you to the banks of the Jordan. A good song can leave you feeling what Mary felt. A dramatic reading can take you to the foot of the cross. It is thus possible to create a space where the presence of God is more easily sensed because the worshiper has stepped out of selfishness for a moment and stepped into a community representing God's story. The first step is moving from "me" to "we."

One thing must remain central for online worship to remain connected with worship in ages past: community. From the lamenting exiles forming new practices and inventing the synagogue in Babylon to Paul's letters to secret groups under threat of persecution, the sense of being connected to a corporate group of believers and followers has always been integral to the identity of worship. To maintain this community online, there must be both a concerted effort for interpersonal engagement and also a spoken emphasis on the group identity in order to avoid the privatization of the faith. N. T. Wright calls self-centered worship "P-worship—the Platonic vision of 'the flight of the alone to the alone,'" citing that in a virtual world we can easily become "just a group of like-minded individuals pursuing our arcane private hobby."[35] In other words, worship leaders should not completely surrender to the consumer mindset that places "me" at the center of everything but should instead emphasize the worshiper's role as an active agent in establishing the kingdom of God.

This paradigm of engagement recalls the "revelation and response" paradigm of worship, and worshipers must be led to respond in some way. This response could be accomplished through a number of practices, both traditional and modern, tech-savvy techniques. Litanies have long been a practice where the worship prompter elicits a response from the congregation, so they are easily translated into online form with words displayed on the screen for people to say. For people not to feel isolated during these practices, the online worship leader could record several voices speaking the response. The same principles apply to congregational singing or responsive prayer. Other means of engagement call for the worshiper to gather materials and participate when prompted: lighting candles, consuming Communion elements, etc. The important thing is for the prompter to clearly communicate the expectations of the worshiper.

REAL PRESENCE

You can always see your nose. Yes, right now you're probably trying it out to see for yourself if it's true. Can you see it? It's always there, but our brains learn to ignore it to focus on more pressing matters that require our attention. Our senses are so powerful at communicating the world around us to our brains that we literally can't handle all the information that our senses are constantly gathering. This is why it's hard to talk to someone watching the game on TV or scrolling through Facebook on their phone. It's not necessarily that they're choosing to ignore you. It's just the brain doing what it does, focusing on one thing at a time.

Our brains have learned to focus, to filter out all the extra information that our bodies are sensing all the time. But are we focusing on the right things? Many a relationship has suffered due to one person's focus on something other than the person right next to them. It's possible to be standing next to someone without being truly present. The same is true with our relationship to the divine. God is always present. But we learn to ignore God. We let our focus be drawn to everything else, one momentary distraction at a time. Many people feel "closer" to God in a worship service, but that's not necessarily because God is any more or less present in those gatherings. It's because we choose to focus on God in those transforming moments. And when we choose to direct our full attention to God, we can suddenly become aware of how God has been present with us all along.

The author of Hebrews tells us we "have not come to something that can be touched, a blazing fire, and darkness, and gloom, and a tempest" (12:18). Yet it's something that is still there. God's presence is real and powerful, waiting for us to seek it and unlock something new. But if you don't go looking for it, you might miss it altogether.

Poet Gerard Manley Hopkins wrote around the time that electricity was just beginning to be widely used. In "God's Grandeur," Hopkins compares God's presence to an electric current, something that is there but can't be seen unless its powerful energy arcs out occasionally with a bright flash. All that stored-up energy is waiting for somewhere to go.

> The world is charged with the grandeur of God.
>   It will flame out, like shining from shook foil;
>   It gathers to a greatness, like the ooze of oil
> Crushed. Why do men then now not reck his rod?
> Generations have trod, have trod, have trod;
>   And all is seared with trade; bleared, smeared with toil;

And wears man's smudge and shares man's smell: the soil
Is bare now, nor can foot feel, being shod.

And for all this, nature is never spent;
    There lives the dearest freshness deep down things;
And though the last lights off the black West went
    Oh, morning, at the brown brink eastward, springs—
Because the Holy Ghost over the bent
    World broods with warm breast and with ah! bright wings.[36]

You can be the conduit through which God's electricity flows. But you have
to wake up to the presence of God. The light won't come on unless you flip
the switch.

CHAPTER 3

THE WORSHIPER'S JOURNEY: JOSEPH CAMPBELL AND SUNDAY MORNINGS

Every story is a journey, and so it is with worship. Author Joseph Campbell categorized a pattern that we humans instinctively use when we tell a story. It all starts with a *Call to Adventure*, a task or mission that only your hero (the protagonist of the story) can fulfill. The hero must *Cross a Threshold* into an unknown world and navigate the *Challenges* of life there, attempting to prove their worth and sharpen skills along the way. There are *Helpers* (for example, the nine members of the Fellowship of the Ring in the *Lord of the Rings*) and *Mentors* (ex., Yoda in the Star Wars films) to guide the hero through these ordeals, but the hero must face the *Final Ordeal (Ultimate Challenge)* alone. The hero is reborn with an upgraded outlook on life on the other side of this challenge, and the road back home is marked by the hero's revitalizing influence, which transforms life as everyone knows it in that community.[37]

What does this have to do with worship? Thinking of your worshiper as the hero and yourself as the guide can unlock your creative potential for crafting worship with a purpose and a vision. By itself, worship is transformative in that your worshipers encounter a word (message) that issues a challenge, and, having engaged with this challenge, they walk away changed for better or worse (you hope they will heed your call, but you know some will reject it). They are not the same people at the end of worship as they were at the beginning, even if this is true only on a micro scale. To craft worship with the journey analogy in mind helps to maximize the potential for transformation, enhancing the experience so that it has the most impact. There can be a fine line between enhanced worship practices and emotional manipulation, but if crafted with deliberate integrity, worship can subtly draw worshipers into a (biblical) story, and they'll walk away with something special to offer the world in the name of building the kingdom of God.

Crossing the Threshold into the World of Worship

To enter the church is to seek sanctuary from the world outside. In a sense, we are leaving behind the familiar, the status quo, and entering the world of worship. How does your church facilitate this process? Are there greeters stationed at every door? Are they trained or coached? How are they trained? What are they coached to say? How do they interact with familiar people and with guests? Even the briefest interaction can have an impact on the overall experience. A warm smile versus a smug "don't bother me" demeanor can make all the difference. How might a warm personal welcome be accomplished during an online service? There is the unique opportunity in online worship for the pastor to issue these words of greeting to everyone. It would not be as personal as shaking the greeter's hand on the way in the front door, but a new welcome message can be prerecorded and broadcast at the beginning of your livestream using a service like Switcher Studio (see chapter 7). It's okay if this message is similar or the same each week, but it's more personal if it's new each week; either way, try to keep it short!

Is there some physical means of marking the crossing of the threshold into worship? These physical reminders are easier to create in person. In some traditions, a bowl of water is placed near the entrance, and the physical touch of water on your skin is a tangible way to mark the entrance into the presence of the divine. Though the COVID-19 pandemic has limited our physical contact, a kind handshake (or now an elbow bump!) is one way to accomplish a physical marker. If your theme and resources allow, perhaps some object might be offered at the entrance to worship: a rose on Mother's Day, a palm leaf on Palm Sunday, a flower on Easter, a rough rock on Ash Wednesday, a tiny Halloween skeleton when you talk about Ezekiel's valley of dry bones, a small piece of braided rope when you talk about casting nets, a rough "splinter" or nail when your focus is on the cross. At our church, we would enter the sanctuary silently with windows blacked out during the Good Friday Tenebrae Candlelight Service (see our order of worship for the service at umcdiscipleship.org/resources/a-service-of-tenebrae). This instantly created a "wow, this is different!" mind-set that sharpened the senses, making worshipers more aware of the worship moment. The possibilities are endless if you have a definite theme in mind, and you may or may not need to explain these objects in detail. Sometimes just the act of holding something during worship can focus the mind.

Physically marking the threshold of entry into worship is also possible with online worship. You might say, "Pause the video now. Go outside and pick a single strand of grass and hold it throughout the service."[38] Worshipers will wonder why you asked them to do this and will be more focused on worship. Preparations can also be made ahead of time, especially for particularly poignant seasons of the liturgical year such as Lent or Holy Week. You and your volunteers could assemble small plates with food for a Seder meal and distribute them for a Maundy Thursday experience. Or provide pieces of clay that people can shape during an Ash Wednesday service. It sounds a bit cheesy to pack a "Worship Kit," but providing a markable, memorable entry into worship invites an atmosphere of attention.

The Call to Adventure and the Call to Worship (including Welcome and Invocation)

The first words spoken from the platform set the tone for the day and declare the purpose for assembling in the room or online. Don't try to give a mini sermon at this point. Instead, consider using a key word or phrase that can tune your worshipers into the theme for the day. In literature and music, this is called a "motif," or a short thematic idea frequently referenced throughout an artistic composition. It helps to communicate the theme with your worship team ahead of time. If the pastor is the only one who knows where the sermon is going, then it's almost impossible for other members of the team to contribute to this technique throughout the service. (Though sometimes Providence does seem to guide the worship leader in the right direction!)

Words of welcome and calls to worship are sometimes an afterthought for the worship planner because they pass so quickly and are rarely viewed as the "heart of worship." But when presented with vision and purpose, these worship elements can have a profound impact on the overall experience. If there is a key story around which worship is crafted, seek language that announces this "journey" at the beginning of worship: "Now we enter the cave with Elijah, waiting for You to appear, O God. We confess our apprehension, but we know that in the cave we fear to enter lies the treasure we seek."[39] You may wish to focus attention with an image, especially if your story involves a known location like, for example, the Jordan River. Decide if open imagination or guided visual references best help you achieve the narrative worship immersion. These images could also be used for social media posts as a "teaser" or simply to put an image in worshipers' minds in the middle of the week.

The online call to worship is perhaps even more significant for the worshiper because there is less of a sense of entering a sacred space if you're simply watching a video on your iPhone. Viewers need to be coached on how to allow the space around them to become holy. Tell them to find a comfortable place with minimal distractions, and encourage them to do something to prepare for the worship event (lighting a candle, saying a prayer aloud, finding their Bible and opening to a key passage, etc.). If there is some preparation required (like gathering materials for Communion, etc.), you might suggest that they pause the video and gather the materials in order to maintain the flow of worship from that point forward. These opening lines are important for encouraging viewers to remain in an attitude of worship throughout the service. Invite them along on a journey with you, and if there is a narrative focus on a story from Scripture, set the stage in your opening words.

Here is an example of language I used as a welcome for an online-only service: "As we turn our lives now toward God in worship, let the worries of the world take a back seat for just a moment, and focus all your efforts to just *be*—to rest in the presence of God today. Take a moment now to pause and breathe deeply. If you need to, pause the video and minimize as many distractions as you can. Allow the space around you to become holy. Come, let us prepare our hearts for the worship of God."

Challenges: Hymns, Offertories, Prayers, and Other Elements

A good hymn has some tension as it wrestles with the state of the world and God's sovereignty, and if we're honest with ourselves, hymn lyrics have shaped more people's theology than any systematic tome or lengthy sermon. Therefore, hymn or song selection should not be taken lightly. It might not be possible to always find the right mix of familiarity, "singability," and thematic connection, but when all the pieces come together, some of the most powerful moments in worship happen when all voices are lifted in praise in concert with one another.

You know why you chose that hymn on that particular Sunday, but your worshipers often don't. To make the connection more explicit, find a way to communicate the hymn's place in your journey for that day. Is there a key phrase that connects to Scripture? All it takes is one sentence to clarify your choice, and you can speak these words aloud before the hymn, print them in the bulletin, or put them on the screen for online worshipers.

The challenging part of these worship elements comes in the encouragement to engage and participate. People make light of the orders in the bulletin to "stand and sing as you are able," but this kinetic act demands more effort from the worshiper than just passively watching and listening. No matter the physical abilities of the worshiper, it is a challenge to be called to attention to sing along with a hymn and join in the communal act of praise and worship through song. The challenge for online worship becomes more difficult to accomplish since it is unlikely they would "stand and sing" alone in their living rooms. But consider what you might challenge them to do. You might focus their attention during hymns by displaying the lyrics, perhaps with images behind them which contribute to the theme of the song, a task which is easier for some songs than others ("For the Beauty of the Earth" is easier than "Come, Ye Sinners!"). If your church does a "passing of the peace," you might encourage them with a spoken suggestion or words on the screen to "let us know you're with us by leaving a comment, and may peace be with you." Some traditions frequently use the "turn to your neighbor and say . . . " during worship. Online this might mean encouraging them to text a friend.

Prayers, as with many worship elements, vary greatly across different traditions. Some groups consider a prayer to be inauthentic unless it is composed extemporaneously in the moment while others prefer a more composed feel or even a physical prayer book. It can do more harm than good to challenge the traditions of your context, but prayer is a highly versatile and personal means of actively engaging in a worshipful moment. Presbyterian minister Cyndi Parr suggests, "I have used slides with a bidding prayer that is effective. I open it with Paul's verse to pray without ceasing and say you cannot do that without walking into walls, so it's okay to pray with your eyes open. You can use general slides of prayer subjects or specifics, such as, a photo of MUST Ministries or your backpack meal program."[40] As Cyndi notes, displaying a picture of ongoing mission projects can focus attention on the community. A prayer experience of this type can be guided by spoken word, a caption on the screen, or a few lines printed in the bulletin.

The Final Ordeal and the Sermon

The pressure is on you, pastor! Most Protestant traditions have emphasized and centralized the sermon as the focal point and "heart" of worship, and this is the moment in worship where all the tangled plot lines come together. Whether you say it explicitly or not, this is the chance to prove why that song mattered, why that Scripture was chosen, why the worshipers picked up that rock on the way in the door (or, if they're joining online, why they paused the video to get one from outside or go find the one you had them pick up as part of a "worship kit" that week). There should be some tension in this message. There should be a challenge. It should not be possible to walk away from hearing it and still be the same person you were when you walked in the door. No pressure, right?

The Road Back Home and the Time of Response

The "Exit" sign is the most holy installation in any church.[41] The invitation. The hymn of response. The benediction. No matter what you call it, the last thing people hear from you before the end of the service should be a call to action of some kind. Summarize why you were all there, and tell your congregation to "Go from this place to seek and serve the Lord" (or insert your motif here!). Physical signs can also be placed at the doors with either a permanent message or one that changes with each sermon or sermon series. I've heard of churches with signs at the door reading, "After worship, the service begins!" You can certainly adapt this to online worship with text on the screen or a prerecorded message that encourages a response specific to that Sunday's message. Online worshipers would feel more personal connection if the service cut away from the live-stream with a message specifically addressing them: "Thank you so much for joining us online today and connecting with us in this way. Your presence here reminds us that we might lead lives of worship wherever we are, not just inside the doors of the church. Wherever you go, God is there. You've heard a message today about [insert theme], and now it's your job to [insert response]. And as you now click away, 'Go from this place to seek and serve the Lord.'"

In Campbell's "hero's journey" paradigm, the hero receives some "boon" or "treasure," and this can be a special object or special knowledge, but the point is that this one thing makes all the difference in how the hero reshapes or transforms the self and the world. Worship offers this in the form of God's revelation, but worshipers need help in order to understand what they must do with it.

Reflection: The Path of Faith

I used to drive a lot. A daily, one-way, fifty-mile commute seemed like no big deal, and that was before GPS told me what to do. Today we let our smartphones guide us around the traffic jams and find the best path. Back then was a different story. Experience is what told me where to go. I got it wrong all the time, but then I learned and made adjustments. If you get caught once at a particularly bad bottleneck, you'll never do it again. I learned the patterns. I could tell where I needed to go based on where I'd already been. I learned.

Then I got a smartphone and moved to a new city. Suddenly I was dependent. Suddenly I found myself turning on my GPS just to get to the grocery store.

Faith is a journey. There are roadblocks. There are traffic jams. There are freeways and rush hour and road-rage-fueled arguments and detours. But there's also a GPS way to do it, one that steers you around the traffic and sets you on the best path possible.

The author of Hebrews knew how to learn the path. Personal experience is probably the greatest teacher, but if you're smart, you'll learn from other people's mistakes too. If ten people trip in front of you, you'd better change your approach if you don't want to fall too. In Hebrews 11, the author catalogs all those "giants" of the faith as immortalized in the Hebrew Bible (what we call the Old Testament): Noah, Abraham, Moses, Joshua, Samson, Gideon, David, Daniel. If you look at the finer details of their stories, nothing was easy. Many of them suffered greatly. Many of them had a dark side and had tremendous moral failings. But something kept them going: faith.

In chapter 11 alone, the book of Hebrews uses the phrase "by faith" nineteen times. If I learned anything from my days as a literature teacher, it's that if the author repeats something a lot, they want it to sink in. In Greek, there's no word for "by" in these verses. Instead, the word is understood by the Greek ending of the word "faith." You could just as easily use a different word in front of it: in faith, through faith, with faith, by means of faith, enabled because of faith, etc.

We're not promised a smooth path. But by faith, through faith, and with faith, we can find a way. We can persevere. Just. Keep. Going. Stay the course. And "learn to lay aside every weight" (Heb 12:1) that drags you down and holds you back. Because trust me: the traffic jams are coming.

Our "normal" gets invaded by all kinds of things—a pandemic, the loss of a job, a new assignment at work, a new boss, a death in the family. Each of these is a challenge, but if we learn to see these invasions as a call to adventure, our lives can take on a renewed vitality and significance. We are the hero of the story. We're hiding with Moses while the angel of death creeps through town, unknown and unseen. We're waiting in the cave with Elijah for the Lord to appear. We're shouting with Joshua as the walls of Jericho come crashing down. We're standing with David as the dust clears and the giant lies defeated on the ground.

That's where the commonality ends. We've all been called into this life of adventure and challenge, but we're all at different stages along the journey. For some, rock bottom happened years ago, and they're on the road back to some kind of new life. Some are still looking for friends and mentors to help them make sense of it all. For some, even a global problem like the pandemic is a smaller test compared to the bigger challenge of chronic systemic racial injustice. We're all in the same storm, but we're not all in the same boat.

So what's the point?

We find inspiration in the stories of those who have overcome, in the heroes of the past who fought the good fights and kept the faith. We glean wisdom from our guides who try to shine a light on which path to take. We find solidarity and courage in our friends who walk this path with us. We find comfort knowing that a better, upgraded reality awaits us on the other side.

The journey has begun. We have to keep going.

CHAPTER 4

WORSHIP AND THE HEBREW BIBLE

Would the Israelites have followed Moses through the wilderness without the tangible representation of God's presence in the ark of the covenant? This chapter explores humanity's need for concrete symbols of the spiritual to guide our attention and focus. Visual online media offer the unique opportunity for worship leaders to focus the worshiper's attention because they control what appears on the screen. The key is to understand the possible distractions people encounter when worshiping at home and to modify the service so that distractions are minimized.

In spite of the centrality of worship for Christian life in a modern world, biblical prescriptions are surprisingly scarce when it comes to outlining specifically *Christian* practices. In the Hebrew Bible (or Old Testament), there are far more stories of theophany (a visible manifestation of the divine such as the burning bush, fire from heaven, etc.) than of worship practices. Although these theophanies represent an authentic divine encounter, they should be distinguished from the divine encounter that occurs within the context of a congregational worship service.

In the Hebrew Bible, there is a strong association between the act of worship and sacrifice. The overwhelming list of instructions outlined in Exodus and Leviticus enumerated the step-by-step worship practices for sacrifices that were performed "for either 1) special occasions; 2) special petitions (let's get God on our side before we go to battle); or 3) atonement/covering for becoming *tame'* (Hebrew term for unclean)."[42] While sacrifice was not the only form of worship, it nonetheless held a prominent role in worship when it occurred. At other times, building a shrine (or altar) to commemorate an act of God became an act of worship (Jacob in Genesis 35 or Joshua's "Ebeneezers" ["stones of help"] in Joshua 4). One might conclude that the dominant modes of worship for the Hebrew patriarchs would look much different than our singing and sermons of today, and many of these worship practices required extensive physical action to accomplish. The books of Moses abound with explicit instructions for animal sacrifices, tabernacle procedures, and law codes for ethical behavior. From the amount of time spent on laws, one might reach the conclusion, as did the Apostle Paul in Romans 12:1, that we are to worship with the way we live our lives—that we are "to present [our] bodies as a living sacrifice."

Worship as Theological Event: The Dialogue of Revelation and Response in Isaiah 6–8

Although Isaiah recounts an individual experience, a vision of God in the temple, the passage illustrates the revelation/response pattern of worship that can inform worship practices for a corporate gathering.[43] The back-and-forth rhythm imitates the flow of a dialogical worship gathering. First, Isaiah "saw the LORD . . . high and lofty," and there was a declaration of God's holiness and glory (Isa 6:1-4). In verse 5, Isaiah responds with contrition, recognizing his own sin, and he is moved to confession. Pardon is issued with the image of a live coal from the altar touching his lips (v. 5), and in response to the question "Whom shall I send?" Isaiah commits himself with the response, "Here am I, send me!" Here is the dialogical paradigm in its entirety:

> Revelation: Isaiah "saw the Lord" (vv. 1-4)
> *Response*: In light of God's holiness, Isaiah's response was one of contrition, as he recognized his own sinfulness—and that of the surrounding culture—and was moved to confession (v. 5).
> Revelation: Pardon for sin is symbolized by a seraph touching Isaiah's lips with a live coal taken from the altar. Then the "voice of the Lord" issued a call to service (vv. 6-8a).
> *Response*: Isaiah responded in commitment (v. 8b)
> Revelation: The "voice of the Lord" provided instructions regarding the mission (vv. 9-10).
> *Response*: Isaiah asked for clarification of the terms—"How long, O Lord?" (v. 11a)
> Revelation: The "voice of the Lord" provided greater specificity . . . (vv. 11b-13).
> *Response*: [Isaiah goes on to fulfill the call in later chapters,] with additional occasions of revelation ("the Lord said to me," 8:1) and response ("and I went," 8:3).[44]

Notice the final response is to fulfill a call to action that cannot be accomplished immediately. Isaiah must walk away and fulfill the call with how he lives his life, much like the worshipers must do as they leave the sanctuary. What's different here is that Isaiah challenges the initial revelation to make sure he gets it right. It is Isaiah's questioning and clarification that is "often overlooked in pious talk about worship and discipleship."[45] Perhaps we have work to do in cultivating an openness to Isaiah's inquisitive nature.

Regardless of whether worship leaders are aware of it, they regularly construct narrative theological events as prescribed by Isaiah. Much like Joseph Campbell in his "hero's journey" (see chapter 3 above), we create a space where the worshiper leaves the familiar, crossing the threshold into the sacred where they are confronted with a struggle (usually regarding the truth), getting help and mentorship along the way, in order to find some new boon with which to return to the outside world. With an upgrade, they are ready to face the next challenge. The medium through which the worshiper undertakes this journey is the divine narrative or a Christian liturgy that "is fundamentally an act of memory or *anamnesis*, an act of rehearsing God's actions in history: past and future, realized and promised."[46] Although one may be surprised by a divine encounter in unexpected places, maintaining an expectant attitude and cultivating anticipation among worshipers is essential in order for worshipers to recognize the divine encounter when it occurs and know how to respond.

Our modern consumer culture creates an expectation that worship is just another thing to attend or, in the case of the social distancing of the COVID-19 pandemic, just another thing to watch on a screen. With this mindset, the worshiper's role is minimized, relegated to being only a spectator. Kierkegaard's "worship as drama" analogy[47] reverses the direction of the flow so that God becomes the audience and the worshipers become active participants. But this begs the question as to God's role. Perhaps the best analogy is to describe worship as a dialogue of both revelation and response in which the spirit moves and speaks and prompts the actors in a divine interaction where no one is merely a spectator.

To craft worship experiences that follow this pattern, subtle language cues can remind worshipers of what is taking place. Before a hymn, the worship pastor might recite a verse related to the hymn and say, "We read in Psalms that . . . and so we respond with praise as we stand and sing hymn number . . . ." Responsive readings and litanies are also a powerful way to demonstrate this revelation and response dialogue, providing the leader a chance to assume the voice of God by quoting Scripture and then prescribing a response which the congregation intones together. Even the brief response after reading Scripture accomplishes the dialogical pattern:

> Leader: The word of God for the people of God.
> All: Thanks be to God.

My church prints "Hymn of Response" in the bulletin for the final song after the sermon, and as worship pastor, I seek to find a hymn that encapsulates the message in song. Finally, the benediction is a powerful moment where the pastor might summarize the revelation offered during the service, and close with a word of instruction about how to go and serve the Lord based on the day's message. In other words, the benediction should provide explicit instructions on how to respond to God's revelation.

The Sabbath

Perhaps the best demonstration of the intended purpose of the Sabbath is a ship (and there is some irony in that *ship* is part of the word *worship*). In the earliest known versions of the practice, there was little to no association between the Sabbath and worship, but the Sabbath's central location in the decalogue and the Torah gradually evolved into a more elaborate practice of ritual. The linguistic etymology of the words can illuminate the distinctions:

> The Hebrew noun "sabbath" is related to the verb *shabat*, meaning "to cease, stop, interrupt." The sabbath involves breaking into the routine, interrupting what is presumed normal, periodically stopping us in our tracks in order to return us to a healthy rhythm of worship and work, a balance between focusing on God and focusing on others, an equilibrium between caring for our own basic needs and caring for God's whole creation.[48]

This contrasts with the Hebrew for worship, *abodah*, which is from *abad*, meaning "to labor or to serve," lending to the more accurate rendering "the service of God."[49]

The concepts seem to be at odds with the ideas of Sabbath focusing on stopping and worship focusing on serving, but one can imagine a balance where self-service is paused for God-service. But the two should influence one another in that "Obedience to God's will should follow the feeling of awe and reverence for God."[50] Hence we are ascribing worth to God by doing something worthwhile for humanity (see the "Love God; Love people" paradigm from the Law and later quoted by Jesus). The English word "worship" comes from the Old English for "worth ship," meaning that you are conveying "worth," or value, to something—in this case to God. In Spanish, there's a connection to "adoration." We get our word "liturgy" from the Greek words for "work" and "people," an act performed to benefit the community. The German word for worship puts together "God" and "service"[51]—again defined as something done for others, not just a meeting with songs and a sermon. Other words for worship in Spanish, French, and Italian are connected to the cultivation of the earth and, by extension, the nurturing of faith, community, and relationship with God. When viewed this way, the concept seems to imply a connection between service for God and service for people. We are ships carrying worth to God by serving other people. The ship imagery denotes not only passage to another place but also a sanctuary from the storms outside:

> The community of Jesus' disciples gathered in a boat was for the early church a common symbol of Christians gathered in community for worship. Even today the inside architecture of many church buildings represents an inverted boat or ship. The image also recalls the story of Noah and the ark, with Noah's family being saved from the raging floods of Genesis 6–9. The Noah narrative is the story of another new creation. This same divine power to create, tame chaos, and bring sabbath rest is evident here in Jesus, who both rests and acts in power to save. Rest, peace, calm—creation's seventh day offers to worshipers a sabbath refuge from the winds, storms, and waves that buffet our workdays and threaten to throw us off balance or even drown us in the waters of chaos. The sabbath and sabbath worship are first of all about God's coming down into our lives and communities to act, to create, to calm, and to give rest. Sabbath worship is an interruption in human time whereby God becomes revealed and present in power among a gathered community of faith.[52]

This disruption of our daily liturgy for sacred liturgy and rest serves to realign our priorities and our vision for our purpose and mission in the world. In other words, for an hour each week, we turn away from ourselves and reorient our lives to God. The combination of both resting and acting, as mentioned above, reveals the concomitant goals of the Sabbath: to express our love to God and to be recharged so that we might learn and seek new ways to love our neighbor.

The Tabernacle and Temple

Not much is known about worship practices during the captivity in Egypt, but as the Moses narrative develops, so does the enumeration of stringent rules regarding the worship of God. Its beginnings in the desert wilderness are polemical: "Thou shalt have no other gods before me" (Exod 20:3, KJV). Even though the Israelites had similarities with their surrounding cultures, many of the practices commanded by God sought to distinguish the people from their neighbors. These practices grew in complexity: first, simple sacrifices at open altars on mountains or elsewhere outdoors; then a mobile tabernacle with an entire tribe of attendants; and, finally, a fixed temple with an elaborate system of rituals marking a place of pilgrimage and worship for an ever-expanding group of followers.

Animal sacrifice was the predominant mode of worship, creating a dramatic sensory experience: the sounds of the priest's words and the cries of the animal in distress, the sight and smell of the blood, and in some circles the actual eating of parts of the cooked animal. The ark of the covenant was a physical symbol of God's presence, including a jar of manna and its implications for both sabbath and worship:

> The jar of manna is a visible sign in worship "before the LORD" of God's gracious gift of food, the equality of all before God, the character of the sabbath as a special day to lean back in trust into the comforting arms of God, and the trustworthiness of God to "give us this day our daily bread."[53]

The visual reminders of both God's intended order for our lives (the tablets of the decalogue) and God's provision for our sustenance (the manna) serve to keep God's people focused on God in worship.

The Exile

"How can we sing the LORD's song in a strange land?" (Psalm 137:4)

What remains of worship when all senses of *normal* are removed is a question that connects us most directly with the period of the Babylonian Exile, especially in times of crisis like a community tragedy or global pandemic. Jerusalem had been firmly established as a center for worship by Isaiah (Isa

31:5). Crisis seems to have a purging/purifying effect on practices across all walks of life, forcing people to focus on what is most significant in order to take the next step and survive. Therefore, crisis provides an opportunity for growth. With the center of worship lost because Judah was in exile in Babylon, worship needed a new center. The temple was replaced by the synagogue out of necessity, and animal sacrifice was replaced by more in-depth focus on Torah and other written word.[54] Even the return from exile and the rebuilding of the temple could not erase the new changes formed in exile.

Distinctions

It would be a mistake to attempt a uniform characterization and call it "Old Testament Worship" because practices varied greatly by geographic region, community, and time period. However, as Dr. David Garber notes, it is possible to make several distinctions

> between pre-exilic worship (which involved the temple but was not restricted to it); exilic worship (where Sabbath really took root in the beginnings of Judaism); and post-exilic worship. In pre-exilic worship, people would not go to temple every Sabbath. In fact, it was impossible to do so for most. Many of the sacrifices would be held on religious festivals such as the feast of booths, the celebration of Passover, or the day of atonement. Most of those were previously agricultural festivals (or aligned with them in any case), and people would make pilgrimage. Before Hezekiah or Josiah, many would also worship YHWH in their homes or local shrines (the so-called high places) on a more regular basis. During exile, which occurred after the centralization of worship under Hezekiah's and Josiah's reforms, there was no way to sacrifice, but that did not do away with worship altogether. Sabbath also became much more central during exile. In the post-exilic period, while sacrifice was reinstituted, the Psalms offer a more extensive picture of what worship might look like.[55]

Tracing the development of worship practices across the storied history of the Hebrew Bible can prove a daunting yet fascinating task. But through it all, it seems that one thing remained clear to worshipers throughout the "Old Testament Era": the worship of God required active participation. From sacrificing an animal to building a shrine to going on a pilgrimage to lying prostrate on the floor, you weren't *worshiping* if you weren't *doing* something. This gradually morphed into a system of small gatherings that more closely resemble our modern worship gatherings today. By the time Jesus entered the picture, there was a well-established tradition within Judaism of assembling in synagogues for "praise, prayer, and instruction."[56]

CHAPTER 5

WORSHIP AND THE NEW TESTAMENT

Jesus, Paul, and the Early Christians

Jesus stepped into a world replete with systemic problems in both religious and political (which were often overlapping) spheres. His ministry represented a prophetic challenge to these systems by means of speaking truth to the power structures of the day and seeking to call God's people back to their mission of blessing the world.[57] As a reformist, it is doubtful (or at least unclear) that Jesus sought to create a new religion with himself at the center. One might argue that Jesus sought to create more followers of "the Way" rather than "believers" in him. People often mistakenly look for *Christian* worship practices in the life and sayings of Jesus, but it is an important distinction to make that he was operating as a reformist of the Jewish faith and practices. Therefore, while we find some scriptural examples to follow, Christian worship is largely a product of the Roman church rather than of the New Testament followers of Jesus. However, when it comes to some worship practices, we can look to Jesus for examples, namely his Lord's Prayer, his Sermon on the Mount, and the Last Supper. These passages from the Gospels serve as signposts on the path to Christian worship that would evolve gradually out of the tiny house churches mentioned in the book of Acts.

The expansion of the diaspora marked not only a transition in worship practice for the dispersed Jews throughout the world but also the development of a Christian faith that struggled to find its identity. Was it going to be a new way to practice Jewish faith? Or would it split to become something entirely new? And, perhaps more important and more controversial, who could join? Must a person be a Jew first before claiming to be a follower of Jesus?

In the letters of Paul, we find more concrete worship instruction such as the words of institution for Communion and general recommendations about who may speak (which inevitably and inadvertently led to the perpetuation of patriarchy throughout history), how to maintain community, the role of music, and more. Furthermore, Paul used all the technological tools available in his day to reach a wider audience. He is the model of an adaptive leader, from his conversion to another way of seeking God to his adept use of the written word. Because he was willing to adapt, we have a record of numerous churches adapting to the paradigm-shifting message of Jesus. This was all possible through the open embrace of technology, i.e., "The epistles carried the same authority as his physical presence."[58] Thus we are able to observe his abiding influence over the worship practices of the church then and now. But a centralized and definitively Christian liturgy was centuries in the making, even beyond Paul's immediate influence.

Ekklesia = "The Called-out Ones" = "Church"

What we do know is that the early "churches" gathered, shared meals, sang hymns, and taught one another. The word for "church" itself, the Greek *ekklesia* or *ecclesia*,

> means "the called-out ones" or those who commit to the way of Jesus as expressed in Matthew's Gospel. The word *ecclesia* calls to mind the faithful remnant of Israel whom the Hebrew prophets had praised as opposed to the faithless people of Israel who continued to oppress the poor and to engage in other acts of injustice. . . . They were simply those who had been called out to embrace the way of Jesus and to live their lives out of that conviction and embrace.[59]

The term was used in the Greco-Roman world for any gathering, secular or sacred, and is synonymous with the root of synagogue (Greek for "to assemble" or "to gather together"). It took some time to identify what it meant to be an "assembly of God" as opposed to a generic gathering. The point here is that it was not a *building* being referred to as "the church" (most of these small gatherings were in homes) but the *gathering* of people—that's "the church." This challenges the modern emphasis on the building itself and offers some validation of the efforts to connect remotely in our modern world. After all, Paul opens his letter to the church in Rome with an acknowledgment that he regrets his inability to be with them in person. But he still "preaches" to them through the letter, and if he had not attempted to connect in this "remote" way via letter, much of our Scripture, theology, and practices would be very different.

As the distinctively *Christian* church continued to forge its identity, scriptural accounts of their gatherings indicate that there was equal time devoted to both "practical" and "spiritual" concerns. Breaking with the established hierarchical structures within Judaism, the newly forming *koinonia* (Greek for fellowship, "a common, shared experience") became a time when "[b]oth 'formal' sharing in elements of ritual, and informal sharing of life were part of the *same* gatherings."[60] This suggests a more holistic approach to faith-life than the now widely asserted *sacred versus secular* division. Scripture indicates that the central elements of these early Christian home gatherings (in Luke/Acts and the letters of Paul) included the following:

• shared meals
• the celebration of the Lord's Supper
• a sharing of homes and resources, including possessions
• the singing of songs
• discipline
• the collecting of alms
• reports from the wider church[61]

What we see happening here is a paradigm shift of service—worship is moving from what was once understood as acts of service *to God* to acts of serving God *by serving one another*. We do not see in Paul something so blasphemous as the suggestion to worship one another, but there is a clear direction to see our human relationships as a means of living out our worship of God (see Romans 12). All of this contributes to Paul's eschatological vision of the church as a new version of humanity, living out the "kingdom of God," an idea "inaugurated in the death and resurrection of Jesus Christ" and something the church is charged to express in community.[62]

Abandoned Practices

There is irony in the fact that the modern church has largely abandoned some of the more concrete worship instructions given in the New Testament, which Ralph P. Martin outlines here:

> I have culled from the NT three practices which are puzzling to many present-day Christians, though mandated in the NT: women's headgear

in church, the foot-washing practice in the Lord's ministry, and prayer and oil brought to sick folk. All three of these have a cultural setting. Yet, whatever modern practice is in regard to them, there are principles that they set forth which remain as valid and obligatory as ever in our day—and in every age. These principles are, respectively, concern for good order, mutual upbuilding, and a God-honoring attitude in worship; the call to lowly service on behalf of others; and the need to identify with Christians whose faith is sorely tested under trial, pledging them support in the expectation that God will lift them to a new plateau of hope and faith.[63]

A worshiper with a more "modern" perspective on worship might be surprised to find these actions listed as "worship practices," especially the "women's headgear" one. It is, however, worth mentioning that in an interview I conducted with one church member, it became clear that, to this person, the way you dress for church is an act of worship, a sentiment this person also acknowledged as one not shared by the grandchildren!

The theme that emerges from the New Testament is a stronger connection between worship and service. The word *liturgy* "is from the Greek *leitourgia*, which means public service, such as Christ's ministry (Heb. 8:6), Epaphroditus' care for Paul (Phil. 2:30), or Paul's spiritual service of faith (Phil. 2:17)."[64] In Acts 17, Paul stands at the Areopagus and adapts his message to the context in which he stands. The modern pastor must do the same to be heard in a digital world. It is the natural unfolding of the paradigms espoused by New Testament figures who adapted their message and practices to the culture in which they were immersed. To meet the challenges of the digital era, the church must continue its long history of adaptation.

An Updated Worship Paradigm from Luke: Encounter, Explanation, Eating, Enlightenment, Exit

Much like Isaiah 6, Luke offers a narrative which can inform our worship practices in terms of revelation and response, further illuminating what goes on in a divine encounter. We find two illustrative stories near the end of the Gospel, the first in Luke 24:36-48 can be analyzed with the following paradigm from a sermon by Robert N. Nash, Jr.:

1. *Encounter.* The disciples encounter Jesus. They do so out of some fear about who he is and what all of this is about. At first they do not recognize him.

2. *Explanation.* Jesus explains to them who he is. He starts with his resurrected body as a sign of who he is and then he moves on to use the scriptures to explain who he is and what all of this is about. In the process he opens their minds so they can understand the Scriptures. A powerful word . . . he opens their minds. I'm not sure we always open our minds to what Jesus says to us. I think sometimes we close our minds to what Jesus is trying to tell us.

3. *They eat.* They give Jesus a piece of broiled fish as a kind of resurrection repast and as evidence of his own humanity and he eats it "in their presence."

4. *They are enlightened.* They literally experience enlightenment in the process. Their minds are opened. They understand. New truth emerges for them.

5. *He exits with a promise that soon they will exit.* Jesus is taken up into heaven and they go back to Jerusalem until the Spirit comes to send them out.

Let's review: *Encounter, Explanation, Eating, Enlightenment, Exit.*

. . .

Two disciples on the road to Emmaus. [Luke 24:13-35]
The disciples gathered in Jerusalem somewhere. [Luke 24:36-48]

Encounter.	Hello. Peace be with you.
Explanation.	How are you? Frightened. Unsure. Let me share something with you that I hope will help you.
Eating.	Let's sit down and share a meal. Let's spend sacred moments together. Let's bless this meal and invoke God's presence with us.
Enlightenment.	Wow! I understand myself better now and I understand you better. I'm glad we met each other.
Exit.	(Not just leaving but a sacred exit.) God be with you as you go. Blessings on you.

Maybe you are starting to see the pattern now. Maybe you are recognizing that the disciples' encounter with Jesus and our encounter with each other are simply representative of the sacred thing that happens to us each week when we gather for the worship of God.

We enter. We encounter each other. We encounter God. We are called into worship as our instrumentalists play. This is a sacred encounter. God is here. Other people we love are here.

Explanation occurs. It is happening now. The Scriptures are opened and explained to us. It doesn't just happen for you. It happens for me. It just happens for me or for Justin earlier than it happens for you. We read the text that we will explain to you and we ask for the Spirit to explain it to us. We ask for the Spirit to lead us to sources that will help us understand.

Sometimes we eat here. We share a Eucharistic meal together. Or we go to eat with our families or with each other after. We talk about what we have heard and what we understand.

Enlightenment occurs both here and beyond here. We reflect on the music that was played and sung, the scripture that was read, the sermon that was preached, the prayers that were prayed.

And we exit. We take our leave. A benediction or blessing is pronounced. We say good-bye and we say it with the literal meaning of "God be with you until we meet again." We exit with purpose. There is a reason for our gathering and a reason for our exiting. God is calling us to other encounters. God is calling us to take our sacred encounter here and make it the model for our sacred encounter with others in the world.[65]

Taking our cues from both the Isaiah 6 and Luke 24 narratives, worship leaders may find encouragement for the gravity of the moment for all the "stuff" that happens at church—from the moment worshipers greet each other on the way in until the moment they leave, they are being formed through a divine encounter. "Worship" happens most perceptively when worshipers can sense the presence of God, but the moment of conscious awareness of "enlightenment" (as described above) is only a small part of the bigger picture. It all matters. The encounter in the handshakes (or the post-pandemic equivalent), the eating at the fellowship suppers, and the explanation in Sunday school and the reading of scripture all matter, and they all contribute to an overall worship experience in which worshipers are enlightened by the revelation of God and formed for a response as they exit back into the "real world."

CHAPTER 6

A BRIEF HISTORY OF WORSHIP AND THE SENSES

This chapter explores how the church has always used visual (and other) media to meet the challenges of cultural trends (for example, a largely illiterate population in the Middle Ages). It will also survey the breadth of worship practices in current use at in-person worship gatherings across the globe, examining the role of the senses in these practices to immerse the worshiper in the experience.

Worship has always adapted to new contexts, from worshiping God on a mountain to worshiping God in a tent, in the temple, in the synagogue, in the church, etc. Now the question is how to best create a worshipful space with only a viewer in front of a screen no matter where they happen to be. In a culture with a predisposed consumer mindset, it can be difficult to transition from the idea of worship being "something we watch to something we engage,"[66] a task that was already difficult when meeting in person but made more difficult when the worship service is just another piece of media to view on a screen. Although the viewer could be anywhere, one would assume viewers might create a sacred space at home. Ironically, house churches have been a part of the Christian movement from its inception. Tracing the adaptation of worship through a variety of historic contexts may shed light on how we are to navigate our current context in which online worship is becoming more common. We must begin with an understanding of what worship is from a theological perspective, and then we will examine its praxis in biblical times through our current day. Part of the task of worship in any context is to create a sacred space in which a divine encounter may occur, and the goal is to facilitate a reorientation of the worshiper toward God and a lifestyle transformed and influenced by liturgy.

At the heart of Christian worship is a trinitarian theology that permeates through all of Christian life and practice, from large corporate gatherings to private prayer. In his series of essays known as *Mere Christianity*, C. S. Lewis describes this trinitarian paradigm:

> An ordinary simple Christian kneels down to say his prayers. He is trying to get into touch with God. But if a Christian, he knows that what is prompting him to pray is also God: God, so to speak, inside him. But he also knows that all his real knowledge of God comes through Christ, the Man who was God—that Christ is standing beside him, helping him to pray, praying for him. You see what is happening. God is the thing to which he is praying—the goal he is trying to reach. God is also the thing inside him which is pushing him on—the motive power. God is also the road or bridge along which he is being pushed to that goal. So that the whole three-fold life of the three-personal being is actually going on in that ordinary little bedroom where an ordinary Christian is saying his prayers.[67]

The same paradigm here applied to prayer also works for worship. This trinitarian paradigm applied to worship means that "God is not only the One before us, 'up there' to receive our praise. God is also 'alongside us' in the person of Jesus, perfecting our otherwise imperfect songs and prayers. God is also at work 'within us,' prodding us, prompting us, encouraging us, and even—when we are unable to pray—praying through us (Rom. 8:26)."[68] God is thus present in every aspect of worship. We only lack the awareness of God's presence. This is where the role of the worship leader becomes crucial to unlock the worshiper's awareness of the work God is already doing. This chapter will unlock the significance of the theological, biblical, and historical foundations for both understanding what worship has been and speculating as to what it might become in light of our current context and the advent of online worship.

Theological Foundations

HOMO LITURGICUS: JAMES K. A. SMITH AND A HERMENEUTIC OF WORSHIP AS THEATER

We worship in order to know. —James K. A. Smith[69]

We are liturgical beings. Out of necessity, we develop habits to reduce the number of conscious decisions we must inevitably make every single day. Thus, we follow a daily (weekly, monthly, yearly, etc.) liturgy with the way we live our lives. Because we now inhabit what Charles Taylor has dubbed the "immanent frame"[70] of the here and now, the transcendental language of the church frequently becomes out of touch with the concerns of daily life. This makes the task of the worship leader more challenging as they must bridge the gap between traditional methods (and expectations) and modern cultural preferences. In short, what used to work no longer works in the same way, but few people seem particularly enthusiastic about changing.

The way to overcome these challenges is to recognize the structures at play in the core identity of our worshipers. The church often operates as if church attendance is a one-dimensional transaction wherein the "message" is transferred to the attendees after they give an offering. Then all go about their lives as if nothing has changed. Perhaps the church has overemphasized information over formation. Psychologists and theologians alike would agree that there is more going on during a worship service than just the transfer of information through a sermon. In order to understand more of what is at play in these complex rituals, we must first recognize who we are and what primarily moves us to action:

> We are what we love, and our love is shaped, primed, and aimed by liturgical practices that take hold of our gut and aim our heart to certain ends. So we are not primarily *homo rationale* or *homo faber* or *homo economicus;* we are not even generically *homo religiosis.* We are more concretely *homo liturgicus*; humans are those animals that are religious animals not because we are primarily believing animals but because we are liturgical animals—embodied, practicing creatures whose love/desire is aimed at something ultimate.[71]

Each of us aims all of our life—our comings and goings, consciously or otherwise—toward the ultimate reality for our lives—our best selves flourishing in the best possible way, or *living the good life.* The job of the worship leader is to align that personal version of the good life with the kingdom of God to the point that even our unconscious habits embody a lifestyle fit for the kingdom. We must recognize that human beings are primarily *desiring* beings as opposed to *thinking* beings.

This love or desire—which is unconscious or noncognitive—is always aimed at some vision of the good life, some particular articulation of the kingdom. What primes us to be so oriented—and act accordingly—is a set of habits or dispositions that are formed in us through affective, bodily means, especially bodily practices, routines, or rituals that grab hold of our hearts through our imagination, which is closely linked to our bodily senses.[72]

Preaching good sermons is not enough to realign the worshipers' lives to the kingdom of God. Only through immersive worship that engages the entire *desiring* being can habits begin to form that effect change.

Developmentally, small children learn first by imitating before they understand exactly what it is they're doing. Similarly, worship practices must model the behavior that worship pastors seek to have worshipers imitate. Creating the practice first leaves time for elaborating the understanding of the actions later, perhaps in smaller conversations. In other words, before the *kingdom desire* might develop, the worshiper must be surrounded with the language and form of an attitude of worship not as a passive reception of a message about God but as an active *performance*[73] of devotion and praise. This is to be distinguished from a view of the worshiper's role in the service as merely a *spectator of* a performance. Instead, the worshiper becomes an *active participant in* the "worship as theater"[74] model, with God as the audience rather than the congregation.

So is God passively observing worship and greedily soaking up the accolades? The infinite nature of God's being cannot be limited to such a narrow view of God's character, and this vision has more in common with the pagan, anthropomorphic deities than it does with the Christian Trinity. Instead, God is present alongside the worshiper, prompting praise (revelation) for the purpose of moving the worshiper to become an active agent (response) of God's kingdom work in the world. In other words, "The real presence of God comes with the expectation of God's willingness to be mobilized according to the needs of God's people."[75]

THOMAS AQUINAS

Although he predates the Protestant Reformation by some three hundred years, Thomas Aquinas provides a bridge between the past and the future through his Christian application of Aristotelian philosophy. His observations in the *Summa Theologiae* both catalog and categorize much of Christian life and practice of his day but with the added insights of the Golden Age of Greek philosophy that also speak to our modern sensibilities.

For example, Aquinas makes a clear distinction between things above and things below, pointing out that what we can know of what's above can only be perceived by what we have here below: "The worship of God has two parts: the first—external bodily worship—is at the service of the second—an interior worship uniting our minds and hearts to God. . . . God's truth can only express itself to us in symbols we can sense."[76] This is reminiscent of Aristotle's oft-mentioned maxim, "All knowledge begins with the senses," except in this case it's knowledge of God. The symbols used in worship (bread, wine, etc.) function to connect the worshiper to God's truth, and therefore the primary means of access to God are the senses. This empirical theology, when applied to worship (namely, the sacraments), suggests that the sensory elements of worship are vital for creating an authentic sacred encounter by which God is represented in tangible symbols that are accessible to humanity's perceptive capabilities. Thus, the Aristotelian empiricism is newly christened:

> Man's natural path to knowing things only his mind can grasp is through what he perceives with his senses. Since the sacred realities signified by the sacraments are spiritual things that only mind can grasp, the sacraments must signify them with things our senses can perceive, just as the scriptures express them with analogies drawn from the perceptible world.[77]

This premise underscores the notion that sensory elements are vital to both the worship of God and the resulting empirical knowledge of God that, Aquinas argues, serves to influence our daily lives as well.

Historical Foundations

THE SENSES IN WORSHIP

The emphasis on listening to music and a message as the dominant form of worship is a modern development. Throughout history, worship practices have employed a wide range of sensory elements. From burnt offerings to incense, freshly baked bread to floral arrangements, wine to palm fronds, there is a long tradition of smells that accompany ritual gatherings. The mind may wander to another place, but there's nothing like a smell to remind a person of where they are currently.

The sense of hearing has dominated the worship scene as practices shifted from offering a sacrifice to receiving the Eucharist with an accompanying hymn and homily. The earliest known hymn with accompanying music dates to the third century CE, and monastic communities have long utilized chants of Psalms (the hymnbook of the Hebrew Bible), which then expanded in form and content far beyond the Psalms beginning in the Reformation.[78] This rich tradition of music is perhaps the primary partici- patory element of worship because "Song engages the whole person—voice, body, mind, and emotion—in worship and draws the singers together in community."[79] Other means of active (engaging the sense of touch, kines- thetics, etc.) participation include giving an offering, shaking hands and passing the peace, taking Communion, kneeling for prayer, raising hands in praise, or holding an object for prayer or reflection. The visual arts, iron- ically, have met with much controversy over the centuries, inciting debates including but not limited to the placement of the altar table, lighting, the iconoclasm of Puritanism, the color scheme to renovate the sanctuary, the high cost of architectural artistry (stained glass, masonry, carved saints, high steeples, and more), and the installation of video screens. The inten- sity of the debates indicates the significance of the visual elements of both worship practices and the worship space in order to "convey doctrine, tell stories, and create an inviting context for worship."[80]

THE SHAPE OF THE LITURGY

Just as Jewish worship developed over millennia, so did the complexity of Christian worship grow as the Roman Empire adopted it and even sanc- tioned it, exerting an influence on worship practices for over a thousand years until the Roman influence became less centralized with the Refor- mation. Here the central event of worship was the Eucharist, where the dominant purpose of worship was *anamnesis*, a liturgical event that

> is in this active sense, therefore, of "re-calling" or "re-presenting" before God the sacrifice of Christ, and thus making it here and now operative by its effects in the communicants, that the eucharist is regarded both by the New Testament and by second century writers as the *anamnesis* of the passion, or of the passion and resurrection combined. It is for this reason that Justin and Hippolytus and later writers after them speak so directly and vividly of the eucharist *in the present* bestowing on the communicants those effects of redemption—immortality, eternal life, forgiveness of sins, deliverance from the power of the devil and so on— which we usually attribute more directly to the sacrifice of Christ viewed as a single historical event *in the past* . . . not by way of a repetition, by as a "re-presentation" (*anamnesis*) of *the same offering* by the church "which is His Body." As S. Cyprian puts it tersely but decisively in the third century, "The passion is the Lord's sacrifice, which we offer."[81]

The *anamnesis* or "re-presentation" of Christ's sacrifice speaks of both the narrative nature of worship and the sensory experience, recalling Old Testament practices of animal sacrifice but also reenacting the covenant narrative by which Christ calls us to follow him. Thus, with each Eucharist "we are *there* . . . Golgotha . . . Easter . . . the upper room. . . . Sacramental communion is not a purely mystical experience . . . it is bound up with a corporate memory of real events."[82] The liturgy was thus as educational as it was ritual and redemptive.

The long period in which the church maintained its most centralized structure was not without inequitable worship practices and perceptions. A large urban cathedral could boast far more extravagant vestments, architecture, and golden embellishments than a small rural parish church. Depending on the context, there might also be a range of education in the room. Indeed, by Luther's time there had already developed a marked separation between the intentions of the more learned clergy and their largely uneducated worshipers (not to mention the preeminence of Latin mass even though there were few linguistic remnants in the vernacular):

> Intellectuals endeavored to control the meaning of sensuous worship, deploying a largely Aristotelian framework analogous to what prevailed across Europe, but their ability to establish this understanding among more ordinary sorts of people is subject to question. In the vernacular, people played with the language of the senses, and shaped their own understandings of the sensate in religion. When turning to the Reformation, it is clear enough that many, indeed most, leading theologians, pastors, and preachers retained the traditional understanding of the senses from learned culture: immersed in an educational system that retained Aristotelian learning, it was cultivated as a basic assumption from an early age. It forced Lutherans and, perhaps more surprisingly, Calvinists into meaningful engagement with the positive role of the senses in religion until the very eve of the Thirty Years' War (1618–1648).[83]

If Aristotle's notion holds true that we can only know what we can perceive through the senses, it follows that all of us sense differently. Perhaps this is why "taste" can refer to things like music and novels. What is beauty and art to one person is noise and nonsense to another. This paradigm applies to worship in the medieval era even before the Reformation. The shift toward individualism as opposed to "communitarian or corporate unity" began long before our modern consumer culture could champion individualism.[84] Do we consume the body of Christ for ourselves, or by

consuming it, do we become the body of Christ as a group of believers? The
answer would seem to depend on whom you ask in the medieval church:
the laity or the clergy. However, the Eucharist has remained the central part
of Christian liturgy then and now, and in spite of the wide array of perceptions and understandings of the worship event, the sensory elements of the
mass also remained the central, unifying element of the church for over a
thousand years until the Reformation.

THE GREAT REFORMATION

Perhaps the greatest shift in worship practice to arise from the Reformation is not necessarily a change in form but a change in frequency. Some
records indicate that Communion for most laypeople only occurred at
Easter (or perhaps other high holidays), and, therefore, "Luther's plan to
have laypeople communicate frequently 'was a radical step for people who
had done so only at the very greatest festivals.'"[85] It is unclear what weekly
devotion looked like in these medieval societies, though one may safely
assume that a Christian worldview was predominant in most European
communities. But just because people *believed* in the reality of God does
not indicate how devout they might have been in their lifestyles and habits.
The church, at various times and in various places, therefore, sought to
stamp out heresy. It is therefore possible that Luther's greatest contribution to the faith is placing the sacrament of Communion at the center of
worship practice.[86]

   With his interpretations of the Eucharist and emphasis on Scripture
alone, Martin Luther paved the way for worship practices to develop more
around personal preferences than institutional mandates. The printing
press made Scripture more accessible to the masses, and as literacy rates
increased, so did the diversity of interpretations of Scripture. After all, if
more people have access to the printed word, then more ideas will emerge.
The aftermath of the Protestant Reformation opened the door to a myriad
of debates and divergent worship practices where before there had been
some uniformity, at least as much as the resources allowed. Even a rural
pre-Reformation church offered a sensory escape, "transporting people
from the often disgusting sensory surroundings of their daily lives, focusing
their gaze on the Eucharist, and bringing them closer to heavenly things."[87]
The theatrics and ritual displays were as immersive as they were therapeutic
and educational. In a world marked by suffering, plague, and malnutri-
tion, the heavenly meal offered at Mass offered nourishment and reprieve.
Do the same elements hold the same power today in an entirely different

context where film and special effects are commonplace, and the population is largely healthy and well fed? One thing has become abundantly clear—the church has frequently used the same language but with varied results as to how the worshipers perceive the Eucharist. What one set of ears hears as inviolable sacrament, another set hears as idolatrous. Therefore, the debates raged during the period of the Reformation, resulting in a wholesale abandonment of sensory worship by many Protestant sects.

THE GREAT AWAKENINGS

From its first wave in the 1730s until the dying ripples of the fourth wave that currently resurface from time to time, the last three hundred years or so of faith in America have been marked by (what many have now labeled) the Great Awakening's overemphasis on personalization and individualism. For worship, this means an added emphasis on emotional manipulation, using shame and guilt as a means of coercing worshipers toward salvation and repentance. Although these techniques were successful in terms of the sheer numbers of new converts to the faith, the diminished role of both community and the in-depth process of discipleship resulted in a faith that was as easy to leave as it was to join. As the adage goes, Baptists in particular excelled at "bringing them in" but not at "leading them on." The consequences for worship practices are still shifting, but this era is marked by an expectation for the dramatic, for a highly emotional experience catered to the individual.

Coming out of the seventeenth century, Pietism and Rationalism both influenced the First Great Awakening and its worship emphases on the "religion of the heart" and the "stress on the individual" (respectively).[88] These two movements would not seem to have much in common, one stressing emotion and the other the intellect, but both influenced worship practices to elevate public speaking to a more central role within the worship service, albeit with different intentions. As a result of this new emphasis, a modern trend emerged in many denominations where *hearing* a moving sermon was the focal point of the Sunday ritual, with the length of the homily now eclipsing other parts of the service. What had once been an multiplicitous venture with the Eucharist at its heart had now become an event where "[p]reaching was the main task of worship, inviting hearers to a moral life, and to meet that purpose, worship spaces were designed first and foremost to accommodate public speaking."[89] Thus the meetinghouses that had been stripped of their "idolatrous" ornaments by the Puritans a century before were now stripped of many worship practices in order to make more room for preaching. By the nineteenth century, all that remained of the liturgy for many Protestant congregations were hymns and sermons. This reduction of liturgical variety also brought further emphasis on the individual with the popularity of hymn writers like Fanny Mae Crosby, who accentuated the first-person pronouns in the lyrics: "This is *my* story. This is *my* song."[90] Within a few generations, some denominations had normalized this watered-down liturgy so that it had become the *only* liturgy with which multiple generations were familiar, having never attended something like a Catholic Mass or perhaps even publicly excoriating Catholic theology and practice. The irony is that those rituals (commonly referenced as "empty rituals" by some detractors) held far more variety and depth than the more emotional camp-meeting style revivals and preaching that were singular in aim and focus.

THE BILLY GRAHAM ERA

There was a time when, to participate in an event, a person had to travel to a particular geographic location where the leaders and other participants were in one's immediate vicinity. Thanks to modern technology, we can now attend events virtually; as a result, the methods that worked then no longer hold the same appeal as they once did. However, for the sake of comparison, let us examine the high point (measured by sheer numbers of physically present attendants) of in-person worship: the Billy Graham era.

> From May 30 to June 3, 1973, an estimated 3.2 million people attended Billy Graham's largest ever Crusade in Seoul, South Korea, with 1.1 million traveling—mostly by foot—to the final service on the airstrip at Yoi-do Plaza. Some 75,000 people submitted cards showing they made a decision for Christ because of that Crusade.[91]

The subjective experience of sensing the presence of God can occur in a small space in one's own home, but by contrast, standing in a crowd of this size with the attention of millions focused on a singular event must have been inspiring by volume alone.

It is worth noting that attendance at Billy Graham's crusades does not seem to have been hindered by the radio broadcasts that began in 1950, "providing sermons and an opportunity of worship for persons unable to leave their homes for the community church."[92] One might argue that broadcasts of such worship elements via radio encourage in-person attendance, at least for those capable of leaving their homes. This remote option perhaps has been underutilized by smaller churches until the pandemic, when even the smallest of churches began using platforms such as Facebook Live to stream their worship services on the internet.

A hallmark of the Billy Graham era was an emphasis on "accepting Christ" (Billy Graham's broadcast was called "Hour of Decision"), an emphasis designated for these crusades or camp (revival) meetings that was intended to begin the journey of discipleship but that for many churches became the singular focus of worship. The entire service, in this context, was reduced to persuasive emotional manipulation designed to frighten "the lost" into a transactional adoption of certain propositions about Jesus' identity. These types of services, as evidenced by Graham's legacy, were incredibly effective at drawing large numbers to the faith.[93] But at what cost? The fallout seemed to vary greatly across denominations throughout the nineteenth and twentieth centuries, with conservative and liberal factions forming within each group.

BEYOND THE BUILDING: THE RISE OF SOCIAL MEDIA AND ONLINE WORSHIP

Much ink has been spilled over the architecture and design of worship spaces over the centuries, with waves of innovation sporadically dotting the historical landscape. From the beginnings with the basilica that was adapted from law courts in the fourth century[94] to the American experiment in Puritan style to our modern warehouse-like efficiency, the building has been the dominant focus of worship space. But worshipers now can sit in their living rooms while watching Mass in Rome. One might say, "The church has left the building" though many still prefer to attend in person when possible. But the question remains: what makes a space sacred? Although the arrangement continues to evolve in the physical space (from Gothic cathedrals to high-tech screens and sound systems and everything in between), one thing remains central: the "common function of bringing together the people and the message of scripture."[95]

The televangelist has been around almost as long as the television, but video technology and the internet recently have enabled churches of every size to broadcast their worship services online. As a result, many churches new to the online medium are inexperienced with best practices and techniques, and they are often overshadowed by churches with both the experience and the equipment to do the job at a higher quality. Which is more important for the remote worshiper: form or content? Does the message or the method of delivery matter more in terms of engaging the worshiper and creating a sacred space at home?

The church has a long history of employing the visual arts for conveying spiritual content, from paintings to stained-glass windows to modern projections of film media. In an era where illiteracy was prevalent and books were expensive, pictures told biblical stories in a universal way, accessible to learned and uneducated alike, even speaking in places where language barriers might inhibit the communication of the gospel. In this way, online worship has much in common with bygone eras of visual presentation of worship content. The primary advantage is that the worship leadership can more concretely control the focus of the visual material (as opposed to an in-person service that might offer many competing foci for a worshiper's attention). The downside is that it's much easier to turn off the TV, computer, or smartphone if the worshiper doesn't like the message or is otherwise uncomfortable or bored. A worshiper might sit through a sermon on a "boring" text if the service is in a building, but that same worshiper might simply turn off the sermon if it is online.

Worship practices have evolved over millennia, but the senses have always played a role in both the revelation of and response to God that occur in the worship experience. We now stand at the beginning of a shift where those practices are finding a new identity online. It is time for the local church to embrace digital means of facilitating the worship of God online.

PART 2

The Practice of Online Worship

CHAPTER 7

THE BASICS OF VIDEO PRODUCTION FOR ONLINE WORSHIP

Here is your practical manual for taking your church online and adopting the best practices to help you thrive in your context. Your needs will vary based on the size of your church and the number of staff and volunteers on your team. Some churches may be able to livestream simultaneously to multiple platforms while others may be limited due to resources and connectivity. You may wish to livestream special events in a simple format but then record from multiple camera angles and produce a higher quality video which you edit and release at a later date. The possibilities are endless, and the technology is constantly changing. I have tried to avoid explicit, step-by-step "click here" instructions since both Facebook and YouTube have already changed since I started this project. Instead, I have provided you with broad collection of skills and techniques which you can apply to your specific context to help you craft the most effective online worship experiences possible given the resources available to you. In the aftermath of the pandemic, churches of all sizes and budgets now have an online presence. Watch a few services from neighboring churches in your community, and take note of which practices you wish to emulate or avoid. You can find examples of online worship incorporating sensory elements, as well as updated "click here" tutorials for software and demos of equipment, at SensingGodOnline.com.

The nuances peculiar to each platform are covered in each chapter, with some overlap since some churches may not wish to tackle all possibilities at once. Read this chapter in its entirety before skipping to the YouTube or Facebook specific chapters.

Can you worship in front of a screen?

Before Jesus came, followers of God were asking, "Can you worship God anywhere other than the temple?" The answers to this question varied just as much as the answers to our question today about worshiping in front of a screen. In biblical times, there were people severely limited by geography and finances for whom even a yearly trip to make a sacrifice in the temple would have put them at risk both physically from the journey and financially from the expense. Today there are people with health conditions or concerns, and there is also the faster pace of a postmodern culture where everyone seems overcommitted. The answer then and now was to worship in whatever small gatherings could be accomplished. Rather than the form and location of worship, what seems to matter most is *to worship however, whenever, and wherever possible.*

When the first temple was destroyed in Jerusalem, God's people had to adapt. For generations, they had only known one way to worship, but the Babylonians destroyed their "normal." So what did they do? They got together in small groups and told their stories, God's story. They edited the books of Moses in ways that spoke more to their context, and they wrote psalms to speak to their current situation. What had once centered on sacrifice now centered on Scripture and story. The synagogue rose to new life. They found a way to worship in the world in which they lived.

Kept at home by the coronavirus, God's people have had to adapt. For generations, we knew what to do when we went to church, but coronavirus destroyed our "normal." So what did we do? We kept community alive with technology. We shared our stories, God's story. We preached to empty rooms, spoke into a screen, and figured out Facebook Live. We "zoomed" in. We "zoomed" out. We talked about masks and hand sanitizer and how far apart to sit. What had once centered on getting people in the doors now centered on keeping them safe. Distanced, digital worship was born. We found a way to worship in the world in which we live.

Having lived and ministered through the pandemic, you've already figured out how to survive in this digital world, but you might need a little help in order to thrive. There's something special about worshiping in the temple and in the local sanctuary, but circumstances constantly arise in which gathering with the community is not always possible. It is for this reason that online worship must be embraced as the natural unfolding of

God's work in the world. Yes, there are those who might choose to stay home because of the added convenience, and there are those who will get out of the habit of coming to church altogether. But those trends were happening anyway. Online worship offers a new, fresh alternative to connect with both God and a community of believers. Overall and in spite of its challenges, a hybrid model of both in-person and online services has tremendous potential both for your current church and for the community you serve.

It's easy to put a service online with a streaming platform like Facebook Live. All you need is a cell phone. But how to make it sound good and look good on screen is a challenge. This chapter explores some of the techniques of livestreaming (to make audiovisual content available online at the moment it is recorded so that people can watch and listen live) and outlines the technical steps for making this work efficiently. Ministers can hardly be expected to be skilled in every area (audio engineer, video producer, biblical scholar, public speaker, business administrator, etc.). Hopefully there is someone on your team to whom you can defer when issues arise. But knowing the right questions to ask can certainly help you achieve your desired results. There is often a language barrier between the pastoral staff and the A/V staff due to the jargon used to describe the equipment and what it can accomplish. This chapter is designed to help you know how to speak the lingo.

Utilize Google and YouTube for Help

If you find yourself producing and editing your own content, you can refer to the wealth of knowledge available on the internet. Between Google and YouTube, you can find step-by-step instructions for almost any topic. It's just a matter of choosing the right search terms and having time to look through the results.

Starting Tips

- Use a tripod for your smartphone or other video camera.
- Upgrade your internet service.
- Connect your smartphone or video camera to the soundboard for better audio.
- Use additional media (photos, graphics, video clips, slides, camera angles, etc.) to keep your audience engaged. If possible, change shots or text or camera angles around every three seconds.

Ideally, you will have a team of volunteers or paid staff to operate the video and lights in your church and a separate team to operate the livestream. But your staff may be limited, or perhaps you are the only paid staff member at the church. Be creative with the resources you have. The odds are that someone in your church already has an interest in audio/video work or can pick up these skills quickly. Utilize your available resources. If a single cell phone in the back of the room is all you have to work with, make the most of what you have. But spend at least enough money to buy a tripod, and move the cell phone close to the pulpit so that the video looks and sounds as good as possible. You can be discreet for those who are present in the room while still providing a better experience for those at home.

Pacing

The next time you watch something on TV, count the number of seconds that the camera stays on one subject before shifting to another angle or view or another subject entirely. It's likely you've never noticed that media will change shots every one to three seconds. Scientists still aren't exactly sure what this is doing to the human brain, but research suggests that frequent internet use can indeed alter brain function.[96] Depending on the level of use, this translates into a suggestion that technology has, in one way or another, (physically and/or socially) altered what it means to be human.

Because we already inhabit the world of digital media, we must learn to see the water in which we swim in order to navigate it more fluidly. Fish can sense the eddies in the current behind rocks and use it to their advantage, and while the predatory fish analogy shouldn't exactly apply to ministers, if we (the church) are going to survive, we must learn to success-fully navigate these waters (digital media). The simple truth is that when you are preaching to viewers watching you on a screen, it doesn't matter how good your words are; your worshipers' minds will wander if there's not something captivating their attention. Explore ways to vary the image on the screen and instruct your team to switch images as often as possible to create a balanced pace which isn't distracting but still captures and holds attention.

Options for keeping up the pace of the video include:
- Having a camera operator follow the speaker as they walk about the platform
- Having multiple cameras placed throughout the room and a video "switcher" to switch between camera angles
- Incorporating slides and images as part of the presentation

Multi-camera Setup

The simplest solution to keep the images switching is to set up a multi-camera workstation. There are a number of options for accomplishing this goal, but you must operate within your budget. The option with which I'm most familiar is called Switcher Studio, a paid subscription that allows you to livestream multiple camera angles to Facebook and other platforms using iPhones. Other options include some open-source (free) software like OBS Studio for Mac or PC, or paid services like Boxcast or other apps in the Apple or Android app stores for mobile devices. Live video switchers can get expensive and must use standalone video cameras, which can compound the cost.

Using a service like Switcher Studio allows you to provide a multi-camera feed to your livestream using only iPads or iPhones as your cameras. Volunteers could use their own personal devices positioned strategically (and discretely) around the sanctuary, and they need only to download the app in order to connect to the master switcher device (best on an iPad). Or the church could invest in iPads or iPod Touches with tripods for a fraction of the cost of a full live video-switching package with standalone cameras. The cons to this more budget-friendly approach are that multiple devices bog down the Wi-Fi network, meaning that the lowest-quality livestream setting is more desirable since it will not need to pause and buffer (load) as much as the higher-quality signal. Everyone would rather watch in HD, but if the signal is constantly interrupted to load, people would much rather avoid the distraction and watch the low-quality video uninterrupted.

FRAMING AND CROPPING A SHOT

The first task in video production is to determine what shows up on the screen. This is called "framing the shot." Pay attention to the background so that it does not appear that a cross is protruding from the pastor's head! Avoid distractions like cluttered microphone stands or cables. Once you've placed your camera to "frame" the image, you may then choose to "crop" the shot by adjusting the zoom lens (or if you're editing, there is a "crop" tool which will accomplish the same result).

As a general rule, the best way to crop a good video is to get it right from the beginning in choosing the best spot for the camera. If no one is attending to or operating the camera, then a "wide" shot capturing most of the room is the preferred method, especially if people will be moving around, i.e., not stationary at the pulpit/podium. In this case, the video editor will want to crop the video during the editing process so that viewers have a clearer view of the subject. This effectively "zooms in" on the image so that facial features are more discernible, but if the image is not high quality and the "zooming in" results in a blurry or ill-defined image, then the editor should "zoom out" accordingly.

If a close-up of the pastor or speaker is possible, keep in mind the "rule of thirds." That is, crop the frame so that your subject is either centered or slightly to the left or right with their eyes near the middle upper third. Also keep "lead room" in mind. This means that if your subject is looking to your left, then place them on the right side of the frame with "lead room" in front of them. Otherwise, the image looks uncomfortable, like your subject is in a box.

GREEN SCREENS

This technology, while possible live, is best utilized for prerecorded video such as the pastor offering a welcome greeting (something which can then be added at the beginning of a livestream). Green screen technology was once only available in TV and film studios with enormous budgets, but advances in technology mean that anyone with a smartphone and some green fabric can use this remarkable effect which allows the subject to be superimposed over virtually any background image or video. The image below is from an online Advent worship service where the pastor preached in a prerecorded video from his home. Notice the "bokeh" effect of the blurred background. This is possible through the use of a $50 green screen on a foldable metal frame. I took an image of our sanctuary and blurred it using befunky.com. The discerning eye will know it's the "movie magic" of a green screen, but at first glance it appears as if the pastor is in our sanctuary. Use this method if you are doing a separate service to be broadcast only online or for promotional materials or short devotional videos. When done this way, you can promote your event while working from home, and your background can be anywhere in the world!

Rob Nash preaching for an Advent sermon on December 6, 2020 (https://youtu.be/pTvjFuO8L88). He filmed this at home using an iPad on a tripod with a $40 "ring light" and a $50 green screen. The background image is a photo of our sanctuary that I blurred to create the illusion of depth.

For this to work well, you need good lighting and video editing software, but these can be obtained with a modest budget. For the image above, I edited the green screen effect using iMovie, which comes standard on Apple computers and is also available for the iPhone. Place the image you want to use as your background in the iMovie timeline first, and then drag your green screen video on top of it and apply the effect (see Sensing-GodOnline.com for a video tutorial).

Video Quality: To HD or Not to HD?

People are used to seeing precision images on their TVs, smartphones, and computers. If you want to be taken seriously by a new audience, posting videos in HD is essential. While HD broadcasts can be problematic for livestreaming because of bandwidth connectivity, HD is preferred for anything that will be prerecorded and uploaded to a video hosting site (YouTube, Facebook, etc.). The good news is that most smartphones can both take video in HD and edit it. I find the Mac video editing process to be more user-friendly, though PC advancements have been made in recent years. Use what you have available.

Video Production Equipment

If you have resources to buy new equipment, here are some items to consider:

(1) *Memory.* Video editing takes a lot of computer memory, both RAM for processing and the hard drive for storage. At a minimum, purchase a computer with a 1 TB hard drive and 16 GB RAM.

(2) *Live Video Switcher.* It can save hours of editing if you are able to switch multi-camera views live, meaning that you have several angles all displaying the same thing on one screen, and the operator chooses which view to record in real time, switching between views with the use of a "switcher." Recording material this way also offers the option to add graphics in real time, which saves editing time later. Even if your service is not being live-streamed, you can set up a "ghost" (private) Facebook Live or YouTube account to use as a host for storing your videos. Simply create an account that is not public, and you can livestream to that location. This is the easiest way to transfer recorded material across long distances. For example, during the pandemic, my pastor would livestream his sermon to a ghost Facebook page that was only accessible to both of us. I would then download the video and edit into the overall service.

• *Hardware.* Actual hardware devices for live video switching can get expensive but are preferable if you have the budget. The company Black-magic makes a variety of devices in a variety of price ranges, some with the option to record four camera feeds for editing later if needed.

• *Mix.* Companies like Boxcast offer a mix of hardware and online services.

• *Apps.* For my small church, the best low-budget option was a live video switcher app that could be run from an iPad. We use Switcher Studio, which can connect six iPhone/iPad/iPod Touch cameras wirelessly. The only necessary upgrades are to your wireless system. You want the highest bandwidth (internet speed) available from your service provider and a strong wireless signal throughout your sanctuary (a mesh Wi-Fi system like the Amazon eero works for us).

• *Software.* It is possible to use a computer as a video switcher. OBS is a free, open-source software that allows multiple video feeds to be switched and broadcast to a streaming service (like Facebook Live or YouTube). Or paid software like Wirecast or SlingStudio offer hardware "hubs" that connect to a computer and allow a mix of connecting both cell phones and real video cameras to be switched on a computer.

(3) *External Hard Drives.* If you are planning to edit lots of videos for your church, these can take up a large amount of space in your system. You can delete all your source files once you've published the final video, but there are good reasons for wanting to archive all the material. The cheapest way is to purchase an external hard drive for such purposes, but it's probably a good idea to get two since these can become corrupted. There are online storage options, but these fill up quickly, and it takes time to upload and download large video files.

(4) *Apple Interaction.* Apple products are designed to work well with each other. If you have an iPhone and use it to record a video (now in 4K!), you can easily and quickly "Airdrop" your HD videos to your computer for editing . . . if your computer is a Mac. Airdropping saves time during the importing process, which can take a while with conventional cables or memory cards.

(5) *Smartphones.* Many smartphones will now take video in 4K, a step above the regular HD (which can be either low 720p [pixels] or high 1080p). 4K is ideal for short videos because of the larger amount of space it requires. If purchasing a smartphone for the purpose of filming in 4K, get the largest memory you can afford, and be sure to transfer the files to your computer for editing and then delete the original file from your phone in order to decrease the risk of running out of storage space on your device while recording a live event.

(6) *Lighting.* Many sanctuaries are equipped with adequate lighting for filming a worship service, at least for filming with smartphones. High-quality equipment might require some balancing, which can be at odds with the live lighting preferences, but this is usually manageable if you have a team. If you're working by yourself and filming a devotional thought or promotional video in your office, your lighting is probably too dark for people to see your facial expressions. A small tripod with a cell phone holder and ring light can make a huge difference in your onscreen appearance. You will have to adjust to having a light shining in your face, but the quality will give you a much more natural appearance for those watching on the other side of the screen. These kits can be obtained on Amazon in the $50 range.

(7) *Software.* I prefer Mac computers because they come standard with the iMovie application, which has a user-friendly drag-and-drop interface.

Final Cut Pro is an industry standard for Mac, but it has a hefty price tag and a steep learning curve to master the nuances and fine tuning available to you. If you're starting with no experience, go with iMovie. DaVinci Resolve is available for Mac or PC and comes with a free or paid option. If you are familiar with other (or even older) software, follow the adage, "If it ain't broke, don't fix it!"

(8) *Audio and Microphones.* If a cell phone is all you have, its audio is adequate, but if you want professional quality, run sound directly from your soundboard to your cell phone (with an iRig or iTrack interface) or video camera.

(9) *Video Cameras.* These come in a wide range of prices and require different skill levels to operate. Keep in mind that many of the low-end options do not perform as well as a newer model iPhone, but there are some good digital cameras that cost less than an iPhone yet are capable of better performance.

• The Panasonic Lumix GH4, for example, can take 4K video and use interchangeable lenses for either zooming in or creating the "bokeh" (blurred background) effect up close. However, if you are doing all of this yourself, it takes time to learn how to operate one of these devices.

• I prefer the iPhone because it's the easiest all-in-one device for DIY (do-it-yourself) video production (and it also comes with a mobile version of iMovie, so you can film and edit all on one device!).

• iPads have a lower price tag and larger screens than iPhones, and they also come with iMovie, but the cameras are generally lower in quality than those on the iPhone unless you get an iPad Pro (which also costs more). Our church uses a standard iPad as the control panel and video switcher, taking advantage of the Switcher Studio app that connects wirelessly to iPhones placed around the sanctuary. This setup does not provide high-quality HD video, but it makes it possible for one person to run a multi-camera setup from the back of the room, and you can switch cameras on the fly, which saves you time when editing the final video (you need only to trim the ends). This works for both livestreaming or recording events, musical performances, and promotional videos filmed in the sanctuary or in any location with stable Wi-Fi.

Bandwidth

The first thing to consider when going live is the capabilities of your internet bandwidth. It's possible to go live on Facebook with one bar of service, but the experience for the worshiper can be counterproductive if the stream is not continuous. If you've ever had to wait while a video "buffers" or loads, this creates an incredibly distracting and frustrating environment with much the same effect as a loud baby crying during the sermon or audio feedback from the sound system during a song. So what do you do then? Make sure to livestream at the lowest-quality setting so that the connection stays stable. People are more willing to watch a blurry picture than to wait for the video to buffer (or load) every thirty seconds. Such pauses are incredibly distracting. If that happens regularly, I suggest recording the service and then uploading it to YouTube or Facebook (or both) later in the day. People will appreciate the better experience of watching uninterrupted.

The first step to going live is to upgrade your internet service to the fastest level you can afford, but if this is not practical financially, I suggest recording the service on a cell phone and uploading it immediately following the service. This would at least ensure a seamless viewing of the worship service without the unwanted distraction of buffering. You can Google search "run speed test," and it will show you how fast your internet service is. Ours at church varies between 50-100 megabytes per second download, but the part to pay attention to is upload speed. This is how you will broadcast a live service. Ours can get as high as 48, but I've seen it drop to 0.02 in the middle of the service, and there's nothing we can do to change it at the moment since we have the highest internet speed available in our area.

Audio and Livestreaming

If they can't hear you, it doesn't matter how good your sermon or service looks. Cell phone microphones have a limited range, so place your single smartphone setup as close to the pulpit as possible if that is your only means of capturing audio. Tripods come in all sizes, and a small one may be placed discreetly on a front pew, largely out of sight with an operator nearby.

Consider how to get a signal from the soundboard to your streaming device. If your church has a professional soundboard, there are a number of ways to run a signal directly to your streaming device. Often the main signal ("mains" or "outs") go directly to your speakers or first to power amplifiers (amps) and then to your speakers. But many boards are equipped with auxiliary outputs (or "aux sends"). Your sound technician (or you!) can choose which signals to send to your streaming device. It is important to note that the mix in the room might sound completely different for those tuning in an home. For example, a piano might not need a mic to be heard in the sanctuary, but without a mic, it might not be heard at all on your recording or livestream. Therefore, it is advisable to set a separate mix for the online service. In order to do this, the sound tech must configure each channel to be controlled separately and independently from your live mix. This is more difficult but can be much more effective, especially if you have a large number of microphones in use for a band or other live music. For another example, the drums might not need a mic in the room, but they may become inaudible on the recording without a microphone. You can ask your sound tech to mic the drums and only send this signal to the streaming device. Many volunteers might have only limited knowledge of the soundboard, knowing only how to mute and unmute. If this is the case, invest in a training session by a local professional and work together to discover how your particular equipment works. YouTube is a great resource for educational content. Simply search for your soundboard's model name and number along with the problem you're attempting to solve.

Perhaps the most cost effective way to connect your soundboard to your streaming device is through the use of a device called an iRig (or any TRRS ¼"-⅛" adapter), which allows a signal to be directly input into the iPhone, iPad, or other streaming device. However, these connectors are basic and do not allow for adequate monitoring of the audio level. There is a thin line on the volume between too low to be heard and too loud and distorted to be understood. The best method is to purchase a device called an audio interface that translates the signal from your soundboard into a signal to be broadcast on your livestream.

Audio Interfaces

These devices come in a wide range of prices, but the Focusrite brand is the one chosen by my church. The iTrack solo offers a lightning connector to be plugged directly into an iPhone or iPad for easy recording or livestreaming, and there is a signal monitoring feature on the volume knob with color changing level indicators. As someone speaks the knob will turn green, yellow, or red—turn it while they are speaking until you have mostly green with a few jumps to yellow in order to have the best signal (red will be unusable!). In addition to the visual monitor, these devices allow headphones to be plugged into the device so you can hear what your online worshipers are hearing. If you are streaming from a laptop or desktop computer, the Focusrite Scarlet 2i2 is a good option. There are other devices and other brands, but these are two with which I am experienced, and they are currently industry-standard budget options which work well in a church setting.

Music

There is a big difference in mixing audio for live sound in the room and mixing it to be recorded or streamed online. Many church sound techs are familiar with the live setting, but translating this to a livestream can be a challenge. This is most noticeable in music. Many sanctuaries have a grand natural reverb, the effect generated by the sound waves bouncing off the walls and seeming to linger in the air longer (the length of this lingering is called "decay"). This is what the tech people mean when they refer to a room as being "live," and if there's no reverb, it's called "dead." You may have noticed that when you were listening to music in church, it sounded much better than when you went home to view the recording. One possibility is the missing reverb on the recording. There are two possible remedies for this problem. If your soundboard is equipped with "onboard effects," one of these is reverb, and on some boards this may be added to the auxiliary send in order to give the feeling that the music is happening in the worship space. Audio with no reverb can be referred to as "dry," while audio with too much reverb can be called "wet." You should strive for a medium between the two for your livestream.

Depending on the setup of musicians for your service, you may need to use "compression" (an audio effect that brings weak signals up to make them louder and loud signals down to keep them from being distorted) in order to get an even mix where everything can be heard. Because pianos may be inaudible on the livestream without a mic, this signal may be muted for the live setting and only sent to the streaming device. The same goes for drums or even a pipe organ, which might overpower the live mix but fade away on the livestream. One easy solution is to purchase a condenser mic that can pick up almost any instrument from a distance. These can be discretely mounted on a regular mic stand and placed near the instrument in question.

Perhaps the easiest solution to capturing sound as if you were present in the room is to place a condenser microphone somewhere in the sanctuary where people are sitting. Your sound tech could route only this signal to the livestream during the musical portions, and everyone at home would hear the exact same thing as someone sitting in the pews. But keep in mind that this approach picks up other noises as well (crying babies, side conversations, someone scurrying quickly down the aisle for a bathroom break, etc.). This approach might be simpler, but it does come with drawbacks. If possible, it is preferable to use the resources you have to "mix" the audio specifically for livestreaming.

Camera Placement

Regardless of which multi-camera setup you use, attention should be given to how these cameras (or iPads, iPhones, iPod Touches, etc.) are placed in the room in order to capture the service more fluidly. Bulky cameras positioned in plain sight can be a distraction and an eyesore, making people uneasy and diverting their attention from the message. The larger the church, the easier these are to overlook. But in a small church, every detail is more noticeable.

My church (100 members) first began our streaming with a small, six-inch tripod ($7) placed discreetly by the soundboard in the back of the sanctuary with a 20X zoom lens kit ($20) attached to a donated iPhone that a member was no longer using. We used a $10 iRig to connect to the soundboard and only broadcast the sermon, but our Facebook page saw a steady increase in reach. Many members did not even notice the camera, and we started to see members stay connected while on vacation as well as strangers watching from all over the country. Our numbers weren't dramatic, but this method of streaming increased our presence in the community and connected us with members and newcomers in ways that we couldn't have anticipated. And the entire setup cost us less than $50!

We currently use Switcher Studio with four iPhones. We now have two at the soundboard, one with the zoom lens for the sermon or anyone at the podium, and another with a wider angle for capturing the choir or congregation. We have two wing walls on which we've placed two seventy-five-inch TVs at the front of the sanctuary, and behind these walls sit the organ and piano. These walls provide a perfect hiding place for a cell phone camera mount positioned over the shoulder of the pianist or organist, allowing a full view of the instruments and the instrumentalists' hands as they play. For sanctuaries with a more open setup, a small, discrete tripod can be placed on the back side of the keyboard with a closeup of the musician's fingers on the keys. This is preferable to a zoom lens in the back of the room, which might obscure a full view of the keyboard (but use whatever resources are available to you).

If your sanctuary has no soundboard or space to mount a zoom lens camera in the rear, a small tripod may be placed on a pew near the front and out of sight of most congregants, allowing a closer view of the preacher or speaker.

Minimizing Distractions

When placing cameras, pay careful attention to what appears in the shot. Coils of audio or power cables around the pianist's feet can project an unwanted cluttered, untidy feeling to your viewers that can be easily avoided by tilting the camera up away from the floor. If possible, place the cameras so that any bright lights are not shining directly into them (you want the lights to be in front of your subject and not behind).

Utilizing Your Artistic Human Resources

Every church has talent, and often these talents remain hidden and unnoticed by the community. You can record your live broadcasts and then edit them for republication to YouTube if you have the time, staff, and resources. Even if it isn't done every week, special occasions can warrant the extra effort. This allows members to showcase their talents in new ways, submitting thoughts, quotes, photos, videos, and artwork to be included in the online video. Anniversary Sundays are a great time to share photos of memories. Baptisms can showcase snapshots from the lives of the new believers. Graduation Sundays can display accomplishments in full view without as much concern for time.

When the initial lockdowns happened in spring and summer 2020, I had no idea what to put on the screen because I was having my team send me audio of choir parts that they had recorded with their cell phones. So for Easter, I asked people to take pictures of flowers in their gardens (in place of the traditional "decorate the cross with flowers" worship activity). I discovered that one of my members had thousands of beautiful landscape pictures from years as an amateur photographer. No one had ever seen his pictures, but he started to send me a couple dozen each week, and people responded positively to the "peaceful" effect that the photos added to the experience of listening to a worship song.

I knew that another member had an art degree, though she was not working in that field. I approached her with the idea of a time-lapse video of her drawing something depicting the words of a song. The resulting video of her drawing a cross set to the music of "When I Survey the Wondrous Cross" (https://youtu.be/345ghzwBGh4) surprised everyone when it was used in that Sunday's worship video, but perhaps for the first time it also caused worshipers to pause for a full minute and actually "survey" the cross. Art has a unique ability to move people in ways that words alone seldom can. Find the gifts and talents of your congregation and put them to use. With a little coaching (I had to send the artist a tripod with a light for this particular project), your members can do most of the work for you, finding a sense of fulfillment and purpose in the process.

As for using online art resources, it may be tempting to go to Google and find images and videos to accompany music or insert in a sermon illustration, but doing so runs the risk of litigation if the images or videos are copyrighted. Instead, use any number of royalty-free images and stock footage available on sites, usually for a small fee. This can be helpful if you can't find something specific in your arsenal of member-created content.

Mixing Prerecorded Material with Livestream

If you choose to use a streaming service like Switcher Studio (see SensingGodOnline.com for a demonstration and more information) that allows you to display other media along with your livestream, then you can prepare prerecorded material ahead of time that specifically caters to your online-only audience. Here are some suggestions for prerecorded material:

• *Guest Speakers from the Community or Abroad.* There are many obstacles to overcome in order to hear from a guest speaker during worship, but the ability to prerecord a short video message creates almost unlimited opportunities. Churches can build relationships with local ministry partners and hear directly from representatives on Sunday morning, allowing the congregation to experience a personal perspective that can influence greater support of the partnership. If you send money to a missionary from Morocco who seldom visits the US and isn't awake during the 11:00 a.m. Sunday time slot, prerecorded video allows you to bring a personal message to your congregation in spite of the physical limitations of your relationship. These videos can be recorded by the individual with a little coaching on production ("prop camera up on something and make sure all bright lights are in front of you rather than behind"), or you can do a Zoom interview and record the session to be edited for use in worship later.

• *Bumpers.* These are short pieces showing the church and smiling faces as a representation of who you are. It allows newcomers to get a sense of your personality, and members might enjoy seeing themselves or their families from time to time. Try to keep these at no more than thirty seconds (fifteen is even better!).

• *Announcements and Countdowns.* This is one segment in the live worship service that can drag on for a long time if not carefully managed, but this information can be easily and quickly displayed in an online format through the use of graphics. One idea is to put this information in a "countdown" that starts displaying five minutes before the live service begins. If you have screens in your building, this information can "loop" (play repeatedly) on the screens, accompanied by music and a clock counting down the minutes until worship begins. The same video can be displayed on the livestream and allow people to tune in before the livestream starts and give them some meditative music to create a more worshipful atmosphere at home.

• *Response or Invitation.* The end of your service is typically a "time of response," but this looks different for someone sitting at home who does not have the option to walk up front or even shake hands with the pastor on the way out the door. One way to create more opportunity for response is to prerecord a final word from the pastor with a benediction, invitation, or ideas for how to respond. This could be the same every week or catered to a specific season or sermon series. Be sure to look directly into the camera and address those watching at home. You can say something like this: "Thank you so much for worshiping with us today! If you found something meaningful in our service, let us know in the comments section. If you're a guest with us, we'd love to hear from you. Leave us a comment or give us a call. We'd love to tell you more about who we are and how you might join our community."

• *Reports from Ministry Teams.* People enjoy seeing what church members have been doing in the community. A tech-savvy parent at the youth group's mission retreat can take photos and make a video report of the event to be shared as a part of worship. The risk here is that, without coaching, these videos can become a showcase of "silly selfies," so coach the person ahead of time and preview the video before it is aired during the worship service. Be careful about where the video is placed in worship. If it doesn't contribute to the overall theme and message of the day, include it as a prelude to worship in the announcement time rather than featuring it after a prayer or offering.

Complete Low-budget Setup for a Small Church

Here is how my church, Heritage Fellowship, was able to create a hybrid model for under $1,000.

The most useful budget item is an Apple iPad, which costs less than $350 for the base model. With this one device, you can go live on Facebook in a variety of ways and even record and edit your videos with the included software, iMovie. In order to create a multi-camera setup using iPads, iPhones, or iPod Touches, we subscribe to a service called Switcher Studio for $50 a month, and several members either donated old iPhones or downloaded the app on their current phone, and with this iPad and a $120 audio interface (Focusrite iTrack Solo) connecting to the soundboard, we have a multi-camera broadcasting studio capable of six camera feeds with the option to add text like a news channel, the capability of playing prerecorded videos and displaying sermon slides or images, and it can all be operated by one person at the soundboard. Is there a learning curve? Yes, absolutely. But when we wanted to have a deacon ordination during the Thanksgiving COVID-19 spike, we were able to ask our congregation to stay home and tune in live while only deacons and their family members were allowed in the room.

For Bible studies, book studies, small groups, or other smaller gatherings, it's easy to put a laptop on a chair and allow folks to tune in via Zoom, FaceTime, or Facebook Messenger if they can't make it in person. I suggest getting a small tripod and putting a cell phone near the main speaker for the night. Select someone from the group to manage the technical part so that you can allow the online participants to ask questions. This is because it's hard to see their hands in the air or hear them if you're speaking from a few feet away, but it's quick and easy to relay information if someone near the camera has the specific job of "tech manager" (or whatever you want to call this job).

If you have people who don't already possess this type of technology but want to join, I suspect there are members in your congregation who are willing to donate to a cause like this. iPads are the easiest starting place with the capabilities of having a data plan for people who don't have Wi-Fi in their homes. You can create church accounts for Facebook and YouTube and Zoom, download all the apps to the device, and hand it to the person already set up and ready to go with bookmarks on the home screen for each item. It's not foolproof, but it's the easiest way to start.

For outfitting your sanctuary with cameras, if you have to buy all new equipment, iPod Touches get the job done at less than $200 each. But a much better, inexpensive option is to ask your congregation to donate old iPhones that they are no longer using. (Keep in mind that depleted phone batteries can be replaced and installed for around $40, and we've found that our Switcher Studio app works on phones as old as the iPhone 6s.) You can set up a church Apple ID and use it on all devices.

If you plan to produce your own short videos that are entirely online, I suggest two things: a ring-light tripod with a cell phone holder, and a green screen. There are also ring lights that clip to your desk and hold your phone at any angle. The light fills in the shadows on your face and makes the video look much more natural. The green screen can help dramatically with the background. In Zoom, you get much better results with the light and green screen when putting any image you want behind you. If you have an iPhone, you can do the greenscreen technology on your phone and then upload it to Facebook or YouTube directly. It's that simple.

If you have a Mac computer, you can easily use the green screen tool in iMovie and then upload to Facebook or YouTube. These are great for promoting upcoming events; just make sure you put as much information in the first ten seconds as possible. If it takes you thirty seconds to say, "Good afternoon and welcome to Heritage Fellowship. I'm associate pastor Justin Bishop, and I'm delighted to be speaking with you today," people have already moved on! The average view is going to be around three seconds, so you have that long to catch people's attention and hold it. So get to the point as quickly as possible "Join us for Ash Wednesday at 6pm tomorrow! We're looking forward to . . . ."

You may think, I've put the information in the weekly email and it's on the calendar in the newsletter, but I've analyzed our numbers, and about 40 percent of our people open our emails, and only about 2 percent click on any links (unless it's the Sunday morning video!). So a short video about what's happening at your church is likely to remind people in a positive way as they're scrolling through Facebook before bed. And who knows, they might share it, and some stranger will listen to the first three seconds and hear you talk about how a coat can make a huge difference for someone this winter. You might get random donations from strangers wanting to join your cause. So what if they don't join your church? You've made a difference in their lives, and they've helped you build the kingdom of God in your community. I say it's worth a little fiddling around with the cell phone to get the word out!

If there's no time for video, a quick picture and a few words can also get attention. Also, figure out what the different demographics of your church are using. If you don't have an official church Snapchat or TikTok or Instagram, then you're probably not connecting with your younger people. You'll want to set clear parameters with whoever is managing these platforms to avoid private messages and the like. Ensuring that multiple people have access to the accounts is a good way to keep the platforms safe for everyone. An enticing picture with the dates for the summer youth retreat will get a lot more buzz than a detailed flyer or email. Even a Bible verse with a nature scene behind it is a way to break into the digital world of young people, and though you may not become an influencer with 20,000 followers, baby steps go a long way toward making an impact.

I don't want you to think that because we do all these things, people are flocking to our church and are enthusiastic about everything we do. Our finances have held strong, but pandemic fatigue has affected our entire church life. You would think that with little else going on, people would flock to weekly Zoom calls and monthly book clubs, but you know as well as I do that it's not the same as gathering face to face.

But this doesn't mean it's not worth doing, and as I said, the benefits outweigh the frustrations and downsides.

We don't have a strong weekly attendance at my current church. There was a time when 70 percent of the congregation attended the weekly Wednesday night suppers and Bible study, but in recent years, any regular midweek program has dwindled to a handful of participants. So instead of weekly gatherings, once a month we invite outside speakers with special- ized knowledge and expertise in their fields, including seminary professors, professional counselors, and nonprofit workers. Because we invested in upgrading our digital resources, we can now host presenters from anywhere in the world without the added travel expenses. And while participation has not skyrocketed, it has improved and is now accessible to virtually anyone with a phone. Even our 101-year-old member calls into our Zoom meet- ings on her house phone to listen in. The important thing is offering people the opportunity to connect, even if they don't utilize it every single time. I imagine that once more people feel safe attending in person, there will likely be more tuning in via technology. But it's also important not to over- extend yourself now. So don't try to implement all of this at once.

There are paid services that can manage some of this for your church, but with a little coaching, you can learn or have a staff member or volunteer trained to use the free tools of YouTube and Facebook. I would recom- mend at least those two because not everyone is on Facebook, and YouTube is easy to integrate into your website. (Oh, and by the way, if you don't have a website, fix that right away with SquareSpace or WordPress. It's not going to make people show up in droves, but when someone new moves to your town, if they're interested in church, they are going to Google local churches first. You need to be posting regular content in order to show up on the first page of a Google search, and if you're not on that first page, it's like you don't exist!)

Most web hosting platforms allow you to simply copy and paste your worship service link to a YouTube video in order to embed it on your web page, and if you create a Worship Playlist, then each time you upload a new video and add it to your playlist, it will automatically display on your website. There are other paid services that offer more analytics and options for video hosting, but I'm a fan of the free ones.

Ideas for Sensory Engagement Online

Worship is an intimate, embodied encounter with the divine, and it does not matter so much where you are but how much you sense the Presence of God that determines how worshipful a moment can become. In my doctoral project, participants indicated that sensory elements enhanced the experience of online worship. I have mentioned some of these ideas elsewhere in this book, but I catalogue them here for your convenience. Participants in the study indicated that these were nice experiences "once in awhile," so tailor them to your context in order to avoid the potential for them to become a distraction.

I have been a part of several in-person services where small beads were used as a point of focus, and inevitably, at random times throughout the service, there could be heard throughout the sanctuary the sound of small beads dropping and bouncing on the wooden floors. Consider the logistics involved and the overall effect of the sensory elements. Is it worth the effort that it would take to distribute the materials? How might the experience be perceived as "cheesy" or "childish" (patronizing)? If used effectively, these ideas have the potential to enhance worship, but they also have the potential to distract. I once heard of a pastor placing open cans of salmon throughout the sanctuary for a sermon on Jonah. Can you smell it already? More than one member had to leave, and one even vomited. Remember that certain senses can powerfully evoke responses from members, so be creative, but also be sensitive to anything that might trigger an adverse reaction (PTSD from a war veteran for example). Also keep in mind the diversity of your population and their personal preferences. What might strike some as light-hearted and child-like might strike others as irreverent, so make an effort to include a variety throughout the year as you explore creative uses of the senses in worship (online or in person). Depending on the size of your church, it can be a monumental task to distribute something for use at home, but the easiest route is to require people to stop by the church and pick up the necessary materials, thus providing another means of active engagement.

- Clay for Molding Something as a Point of Focus
  - For an online *Ash Wednesday Service* (which can be viewed at SensingGodOnline.com), I distributed packets of clay to participants and instructed them at the beginning of the video to mold it into something. Most chose a cross, and one participant said, "As I held and molded that clay cross in my hand, I felt a new responsibility for the cross, even though I know I'm separated from it by over 2,000 years. It made the experience more tangible and real for me." At the end of the service, we drew attention to the dust on hands after handling clay as we used the words familiar to the service: "From dust you came, and to dust you shall return."
  - Both the granular texture of the touch and the earthy fragrance of the clay create an experience which stands out (for better or worse) for your congregants.
- *Communion Elements*
  - It is easy to instruct online worshipers to prepare bread and juice (or wine!) ahead of time in preparation for the service, or individually sealed packages of juice and wafers can be purchased and distributed.
  - Bread and juice are the most traditional means of incorporating the sense of taste into worship, not to mention touch and smell.
- *Maundy Thursday Passover/Seder Meal*
  - This symbolic gathering from the Jewish tradition is the meal Jesus was having with his disciples on the night of the last supper.
  - Meal kits can be prepared for distribution, including the traditional symbolic elements of charoset (a mixture of apples, nuts, cinnamon, cranberries, and honey), a boiled egg, a bone (lamb shank if possible), greens (parsley and lettuce), and bitter herbs (horse radish), along with juice and salt water. Find a *haggadah* (set of instructions for the service) online, and guide your congregation through a multi-sensory experience that retells the story of Moses and the people's flight to freedom while

following in the shoes of Jesus on the night he was betrayed, giving new meaning to the bread and cup.
- Guiding the meal online gives the opportunity to include visual elements to aid in telling the story of the Israelites' flight from Egypt, as well as the taste, smell, and feel of the food involved.
- View an example on SensingGodOnline.com.
- *Candles*
  - Lighting a candle at the beginning of worship is an excellent way to mark the transition from secular to sacred space, and it can help viewers at home to psychologically perceive the space around them as "more holy." Show someone lighting a candle on the screen with instructions to do something similar at home (pausing the video if necessary to get materials) and "allow the space around you to become holy."
  - For an online *Good Friday Station of the Cross/Tenebrae Service* (viewable at SensingGodOnline.com), I distributed seven battery-powered candles to participants with instructions to go to a dark room to watch the service, with the only light coming from the candles. As the story of Jesus' journey to the cross unfolded in visuals onscreen (clips from *The Jesus Film Project*, used with permission, narrated by me reading Scripture), worshipers were instructed to extinguish a candle. There are traditionally fourteen stations of the cross, but I condensed it to seven for cost and convenience. One participant cited this experience as one of the most powerful for sensing the presence of God at home, indicating the intimacy of darkness and the action of extinguishing the candles as crucial factors.
  - The season of Advent also lends itself well to the creative use of candles. Advent wreaths can be distributed or events can be held at church to assemble them. I have also witnessed a powerful service for children where the Christmas story was read, and candles for each of the characters were lit and extinguished as part of the story.
  - The sight of flames and the feel of the warmth if you are near a real candle (not to mention the smell!) create an atmosphere filled with a living presence in the form of a dancing flame. Aromatic candles or incense can further enhance the experience but not for people with asthma, so keep these considerations in

mind as you guide your congregation in how to prepare for the event.

- *Object Lessons*
  - Holding an object during worship is not just for the children's sermon. A branch on Palm Sunday, a stick for a sermon on Psalm 23, stones for a lesson on Joshua crossing the Jordan River—the possibilities are limited only by your creativity as you seek to bring the biblical stories to life.
  - For an online *Easter Sunrise Service* (viewable at Sensing-GodOnline.com), I distributed rocks with these instructions: "You have before you a stone, representing the stone at the tomb. Pick it up and hold it now. Allow your mind to go back to that moment, just before the stone was rolled away." I then proceeded to read John 20:1-18 synchronized to images of the story as portrayed in clips from *The Jesus Film Project* (used with permission). Some participants identified this as the most worshipful moment of Holy Week that year.
- *Visual Ideas*
  - Bring scripture alive while someone reads it by displaying video or still images which depict the story being told. This connects you with an ancient form of storytelling on the painted walls or stained-glass windows in churches whose congregants frequently could not read but could follow the biblical stories visually. Keep in mind most visual media are copyrighted. Seek permission for fair use, or seek public domain material. There are also paid sites (like Filmpac, Worship House Media, Igniter Media), which provide footage with a license to stream the media for a fee. This also allows other church members to participate by recording their voices in a dramatic or narrative setting.
  - See Chapter 11 for more.

Audio Ideas
- Online services allow you to better control the quality and volume of music, which can then be used as a point of focus (displaying the singers or still or video images of beautiful landscapes along with the text of the hymns), or as background music while something else is visible on screen. You can record your choir singing (a cappella or accompanied), giving you

a chance to get the best "take" for use in the video. This also gives you a chance to incorporate talent in your congregation (vocalists or instrumentalists), even those who might prefer not to perform for a live audience.

- *Touch*
  - The pandemic reminded us of the significance of a hug or handshake by taking those traditions away from us. While those alone at home might not be able to hug or shake hands, a worship leader might instruct people to "place your hand over your heart and become aware of . . . " some idea connected to your theme. Instructions such as these encourage an active response to the revelation you have provided in the message.

The ideas in this chapter are not practical to employ every Sunday, especially for a small church with a small staff. Implementing some of these suggestions can bring renewed emphasis and energy to any special event. Be patient as you navigate these waters, and reach out to colleagues or cohorts as you plan to try new things. Often a quick phone call to a friend who has "been there, done that!" can save you from a logistical nightmare. And when it doesn't work right the first time, allow the experience to be a catalyst for growth rather than a stumbling block.

CHAPTER 8

WORSHIP, YOUTUBE, AND PRERECORDING

There are a number of video-hosting platforms available, but YouTube is free and easily accessible on many devices, including smartphones, tablets, and smart TVs. There are a number of copyright issues that churches must consider before posting to this public online forum. This chapter explores trends and techniques for editing a worship service video to be more palatable to online worshipers using YouTube, which can easily be embedded on a church website for potential members to find and explore.

While it is possible to go live on YouTube with various streaming devices (BlackBox, BlackMagic, and OBS Mac software are just a few), this platform is perhaps most useful for hosting edited videos of services that can then be linked to a website. Editing allows for copyrighted material, along with any "dead space" or personal information (prayer requests, announcements), to be removed from the recording. The edited video can be in its most concise form for those interested in discovering your church or attending for the first time. There is also room to add "B-roll" or extra pictures, footage, or artwork that might enhance the viewing experience in order to create a more visually interesting sequence than watching the pianist's hands from a distance for four minutes (this can be interesting with multiple angles and closeups, fade-ins, etc., but with one stationary camera from far away, it can become boring quickly, allowing the worshiper's mind to wander and taking away from the overall experience). There is likely an amateur photographer or artist in your congregation, and these edited videos allow a perfect place to showcase their talent while enhancing the worshiper's focus.

Video editing can be accomplished by a paid company or staff member, or generally by any number of church members who might have a passing interest in the skill. Recent iPhones can both capture and edit video, or the footage can be downloaded from a livestream on Facebook and then edited to be uploaded to YouTube. There are also a number of video editing software programs. For Mac users, iMovie comes standard and is more user-friendly while the more expensive Final Cut Pro offers greater versatility but with a steeper learning curve. There are some free video editors like DaVinci Resolve which work on either Mac or PC.

Copyright

A church operating within the bounds of copyright law will be familiar with CCLI (Christian Copyright Licensing International), but it is important to note that a standard license does not cover livestreaming or posting web content. A special license is required to use music online, but it is relatively inexpensive. This does not give a church freedom to post anything they wish. Images and video clips in particular should be given special consideration. If a sermon illustration includes copyrighted material, some platforms (like Facebook) will block the content or black it out, even from a livestream.

The algorithms of YouTube can detect the melody of a copyrighted song, even if it is produced and recorded at your church. This is true of many hymns that are newer than the past 100 years. However, you are still able to use the music but with some restrictions. Most copyrighted songs can be used, but the owner of the copyright reserves the right to "monetize" the video, meaning that they can place ads on your video, and only they can make a profit. If your church is small, the odds are that your channel will not meet the requirements for monetization anyway (currently a minimum of 1,000 subscribers with 4,000 hours of watch time). So the likelihood is small that any ads will appear on your videos, and you are still able to use your recording of the music. Avoid using background music or video clips that your church has not produced because doing so could result in a copyright strike (get three and your channel gets shut down!), depending on the wishes of the copyright holder. You can never be sure if the company will allow you to continue to use their material, and they might also choose to issue a strike months after the initial upload. It is safer to only use material your church has produced. However, you may purchase content from companies like Worship House Media, Igniter Media, or stock footage groups like Filmpac who allow you to purchase their content along with a streaming license allowing you to use the material on your livestream or channel. These videos can enhance the overall worship experience by providing content produced by video and audio professionals. Find one that fits your theme for worship, and use it in both your live (if you have a screen in the sanctuary!) or recorded setting.

Thumbnails

Once you are used to creating content, there will be some content that you wish to promote to a wider audience than your immediate congregation. Maybe it's an invitation to an event such as a Christmas concert or Easter Egg hunt that's open to the larger community. In this case, your approach should differ from that which is geared toward your established community. A "thumbnail" is the image people see before they click on the link to your video, and how you compose this image (and text) will influence how many people see your content in your community and beyond.

Our tendency as ministers is to overcommunicate, using as many words as possible to get our point across from numerous perspectives. But to engage a new audience (or even "on the fence" members who might not be so enthusiastic about everything you are producing online), you need something that communicates as much as possible as quickly as possible with as few words as possible. Be as concise as possible. (Do as I say, not as I do in this paragraph!) Most people use YouTube on their smartphones, so a thumbnail should have only two to three words in large print if at all possible. Less is more. Avoid background images that are cluttered and difficult to discern from a distance—remember, most people will see your thumbnail in a size roughly the same as your actual thumbnail, and at that scale, detail is difficult to discern. If there are graphics/clip art, keep them simple and subtle. If there is a photo, use the tools available to blur the background in order to make the subject of the photo more present in the image.

Here is an example thumbnail from our community "Keyboards at Christmas" concert. A typical in-person performance would likely see a crowd of slightly over 100 people, but this video reached over 2,000 views within the first two weeks of posting to YouTube, and as of January 2021, it has over 3,500 views.

This is a "thumbnail" for our virtual Christmas concert on YouTube and Facebook (https://youtu. be/DP1wZar8VeA). Use as few words as possible and keep them in large print since many users will first see this image on a smartphone in a size smaller than one inch. Minimize background distractions by blurring them out with a good digital camera or photo editing tool like befunky.com.

Photography

It has never been easier to take good photos. Most new model smartphones come equipped with lenses capable of the "bokeh effect," creating depth by keeping the subject of the photo in focus while blurring out the background. On newer iPhones, this is achieved using the "portrait" feature. There may be an amateur photographer in your congregation who would love a chance to help you promote your covered dish extravaganza or toy drive. If you can explain to them what you're looking for, they'll likely do the work for you!

The bokeh effect can also be achieved artificially with computer software (Adobe Photoshop or various online platforms such as befunky. com). This can prove especially useful if you have video of an event but no professional photography with which to make good promotional materials/ thumbnails. In this case, find a frame from your video and take a screenshot (on PC use the "snipping tool" app; on Mac use command + shift + 4; on a smartphone there are various options for taking a screenshot based on the type of phone—for example, on the iPhone 11, hold the power button and volume-up button simultaneously). Once you have your best image, import/upload your photo into your photo editing platform and use the "blur" or "background" options to achieve this effect.

Playlists

Organizing your material on YouTube (or other video hosting sites) can make navigation a breeze for newcomers who are trying to discover your identity before visiting. And these playlists can be embedded in your website, which will automatically update each time you post a new video to YouTube and add it to the playlist. Most website hosting services allow you to copy and paste the link from your YouTube Playlist page and post it as a video thumbnail on your homepage or any other page you designate for worship or other material (music, Sunday school, etc.).

Promoting on YouTube

Once your videos are edited, you may wish to share your creations with a larger audience. YouTube provides a "Promote Video" option, allowing you to pay to have the video played as an ad before a related video or to show up as a recommended link beneath a related video. This is a good option for increasing your presence in a larger community setting, and you can target viewers by state or zip code and also select a target demographic. (You wouldn't want to pay for an ad about the senior Christmas choir to appear on a kids' video!) When my church occasionally produces a video that gets promoted or shared so that thousands of people see it, few if any of these people will join our church, but that type of exposure gets our message in front of a new audience, a message that might spread some joy and make a difference in the lives of those watching. Also, people watching a free event might contribute to a cause (mission project, food drive, etc.), even if they never step foot in your church. They might be inspired by your music or words and feel moved to find a church near them or to make a contribution to your efforts. What would church look like if we spent more time focusing on efforts at work in the world rather than trying to get more people to come to church? This is a thought for consideration, especially in an era when hybrid worship services (both online and in person) are becoming more of the norm.

Embedding (Videos and Playlists) on a Website or Email

One way to help people find your content more easily is to embed videos and playlists on your church website (or Facebook or other social media).

Our church uses Squarespace, which allows a user-friendly embedding of videos. You simply click a plus sign (+) to add a new block, and then paste the video URL into it in order to have the video displayed on your web page. The same is true for video playlists that can be created and accessed from the YouTube Studio (studio.youtube.com, the page accessed by clicking the "create" button on your computer while signed into YouTube). If you go to heritagecanton.com (my church's website), you will see several YouTube playlists that are automatically updated on the website each time I post a new video to one of them. Some (usually older) sites will need to use the "embed code" option to get a YouTube video or playlist to display, but this is essentially a matter of copying and pasting the correct text from the video to the web page editor.

Moderating Comments

One downside to posting services online is the potential for negative comments from someone from the general public who might disagree or take issue with the content of a video. While this can be frustrating and disheartening, some may argue that any comment is still engagement with your material, which in turn makes it more visible to a wider audience. Furthermore, any inappropriate material (profanity, etc.) can be blocked and reported to the streaming service, and comments with inappropriate content can be deleted immediately, including those perceived as "scams" such as the long narrative of someone relating their life story and asking for money. If members or known community members are making negative comments, here are a few suggestions:

• Don't delete the comment.
• Respond with a personal message.
• Thank them for sharing their perspective, and address the issue as best you can, using responses like the following:

"We also regret that option was not possible at this time, and we hope to do better in the future."

"What a great idea! We might incorporate it in future services if possible."

"At our church, we value diverse theological positions. Thank you for trusting us enough to share yours here in this way."

If you can, encourage positive engagement as a part of your video. This can be spoken or a simple text screen with an idea: "What are your family traditions for this holiday? Leave a comment below." If people do engage in this way, be sure to comment back, thanking them and complimenting them for their participation: "What a wonderful tradition!" "That's a neat idea."

If you have a large community or a high profile in your area (perhaps you're the only Baptist church for miles around), you might find that your church is more susceptible to criticism from those who disagree with you. This can be a deterrent to increasing your online presence, but keep in mind that people can easily spot "trolls" or inauthentic detractors online, so one negative review on Google will not ruin your reputation. For example, my friend owns a business, and he has one one-star review on his business's Google profile. The comment is short, saying something like this: "You can't trust this company, so you'd better go with (competitor's name)." It's easy to tell that a person should be suspicious of its authenticity. After some research, my friend determined that the user works for the competitor, so this was a dishonest attempt to undermine the integrity of my friend's company. Here is a potential response to this type of negative online review: "Dear Customer, I'm sorry for your negative experience, but I can find no record of you as a past customer. Perhaps you are mistaking us for a different company? If we have overlooked some of your needs as a valued customer, please give us a call so that we might resolve the issue as quickly as possible."

A few sentences like this can address the concerns of someone who might be looking at online reviews before visiting your church, and your response can play a strong role in establishing the character of your institution. We all know that Christians are divided by many theological differences, and in our current, highly polarized political climate, people could identify you as "Satan's church" simply for ascribing to your denomination's statements of faith. Negative comments don't require an in-depth back-and-forth with the commenter. Instead, direct them to your denomination's statement of faith or to the "Who We Are" page on your church's website. This way, other online users can quickly understand why that particular negative comment was made in regard to your organization.

Sometimes people who leave your church might seek revenge by posting a lengthy narrative about their negative experience on one of your online platforms. It is important to refrain from lengthy or emotional responses to these comments. If they reveal too much personal information, they can be deleted altogether. But if you can leave a comment, keep your response short and apologetic: "We regret the unfortunate circumstances of your experience here, and we wish you the best in your future endeavors."

YouTube comes with its unique set of challenges, but the benefits outweigh many of the concerns. Invest in a volunteer or staff member to manage your channel and website; provide them with as much training as your budget allows.

CHAPTER 9

WORSHIP AND FACEBOOK

Though it is not universal, Facebook is the social media platform with more "older" users, many of whom are more adept at navigating this environment than any other platform. This chapter focuses on engaging and preparing worshipers for worship through text, image, and video posts that make the experience more immersive and participatory. It is important to note that a private Facebook "group" is preferable for sharing personal information while a public Facebook "page" for your church is the best place to post sermons and other videos, photos, or text.[97] Furthermore, while Facebook is a good place to host video worship services, its primary function should be engaging people to respond in some way as either preparation before worship or a response after worship. Accompanying posts with your worship video should encourage actions other than the typical "Watch this week's service." Instead, try to find an action that relates to your worship theme: "Be still with us today." Or "Find the direction your peace is coming from and head that way." Or "Radiate kindness."

Like it or not, we live in a "less is more" era when it comes to information. After all, there is only so much information a person can consume in any given day, so we develop filters that sift out only the most necessary or most engaging (or attention-getting) tidbits of information. For example, the only part of an email that many people read is the subject line! What this means for you as a church leader is that in order to reach anyone outside of your core Sunday and Wednesday crowd (i.e., to reach the "Christmas and Easter" members or the once-a-month attendees), you must compete with literally millions of other snippets of information to get and hold their attention.

Preparing the Field

In an ideal world, every member of your church would watch every online offering whenever they cannot be present in the building. However, we know this is not the case, even if we don't want to admit it. So there must be some preparation in order to maximize anticipation of the worship event or to provide a means of responding to the message. This can come in a variety of forms, such as a Facebook (or Instagram) post with a "teaser" (short preview) of something from the sermon or music that Sunday. This could be

- A meme (picture with a quote)
- A short (less than 30 seconds) video preview of a song or sermon theme
- A simple question
- A request or call to action to prepare something before the worship event (i.e., "Take a picture of _____ and post it here")
- A simple picture with or without words

Facebook offers a variety of means to achieve these goals, and you don't have to be glued to your phone or computer to pull it off. Posts can be created during regular office hours days in advance and then scheduled to run at strategic times when most people are likely to see them: a lunch break, after dinner, or mid-morning on Saturday.

The way Facebook's algorithm (and most social media for that matter) works is that the more people engage with content, the more the platform pushes that content to them. So find what makes people click your link, comment on your post, and share your post, and keep doing it, mixing it up from time to time to keep things fresh. This is called "breaking the script."[98] You want content that will engage people's curiosity and sense of purpose and identity without being too heavy-handed. So less is indeed more. How can you get your message across in as few words as possible? It takes more effort and practice than you might imagine, but it is possible to say more in a good picture and two or three words than in a thousand words that no one has time to digest. In my hometown near Atlanta, one local pastor paid for radio ad time and rarely spoke longer than a minute, but his "Right from the Heart" segments were powerful, and everyone knew his name whether they went to his church or not. The effectiveness of the advertising industry is proof of how much can be accomplished in a short amount of time, so take cues from their techniques and learn to create short, meaningful content in order to expand your presence in the community and get your message heard by more people. The key is to condense what you have to say into as few words as possible, effectively producing mantra. One local music minister sets the tone for the community nature of his choir by the frequent use of the catchphrase: "More than music, we are family!" It might only be six words, but everyone knows it, and it sets the bar high for any meeting of the group. If you can make a mantra, your message is more likely to stick.

Premieres

If you have prerecorded a video, the premiere option on Facebook (and YouTube and probably other platforms as well) allows you to broadcast a video at a specific time so that people can watch "live" together in real time. Some larger churches have discovered that it's easier to control the content, audio, and transitions and to edit out pauses and distractions if they are not livestreaming their services. So they film a version of the worship service earlier in the week to be aired as a premiere at the same time that worship is happening live in the building. This is difficult if not impossible for a small church to achieve, but, if you have someone who can commit to the work, I recommend recording your service at 11:00 a.m., editing out the pauses and anything distracting or unnecessary (i.e., announcements or instructions that apply only to those in the building, etc.), and then posting your service as a video premiere to air later in the day. This takes care of any bandwidth issues (pauses while loading) of a livestream as well as the unwanted distractions of pauses or shaky cameras.

Replays

Many sermons are built around a powerful theme or motif that carries through the message, and these focal points can be isolated and published as separate short videos (less than one minute) on Facebook, Instagram, or other social media. The benefits to this are twofold: (1) those who were in the room might see the post later in the week, and recalling the message might help institute a culture of worship as a way of life; and (2) those not in the room (or not even familiar with your church) might see the "preview" and want to know more. Include a link to the full service in your post so that those who want to know more know where to find it.

Recaps for Small Groups

One way to build community around a common message is to provide structured guides for small groups built around the same theme as the worship service. If sermons are planned and written in advance, then a staff member or volunteer could pull key points from the sermon and draft discussion questions for small groups to use during discussions. If sermons are extemporaneous, then this task could be completed Sunday afternoon or Monday and emailed to group leaders for use later in the week. If sermons are recorded, key points could be isolated and included as videos to accompany the questions. This is time consuming but effective if you have the resources.

Hashtags

One way to encourage engagement and active participation in a sermon idea is to promote the use of a hashtag to go along with a theme.[99] For a sermon series on kindness, worshipers could look for opportunities to show kindness in their daily lives and post pictures or messages or quotes with the hashtag #bekind. A practice such as this gives your members a way to actively participate in something, and it encourages them to make worship a part of their daily lives in some way, if only to "live out" what was mentioned in the sermon or identify in the context of daily life what was proclaimed in worship. Those who abstain from social media can be encouraged to email staff or send a letter to the church with the same guidelines, and these messages could be included in a weekly email or posted to the church's Facebook account.

Playlists

When visitors access your Facebook page, it is important for them to be able to access who you are by being able to find worship services easily (this is true for your church website as well). There is a video editor option on Facebook that allows you to create playlists, much like on YouTube (mentioned in Chapter 8). Name these so that they are obvious and easy to find: "Worship," "Sunday Service," "Sermons," "Music," or "Sunday School." These are useful for members and nonmembers alike.

Short Devotional Videos

Less is more. That's the rule with any online material. Never underestimate the power of a short, thoughtful message. Try to put the best part first and then explain. When viewing videos, people's minds wander quickly, so don't take too long to introduce the concept. Make the powerful statement first, and then back up and explain it. This is true for scriptural reflections too. Give a lot of thought to your first sentence, and then you can read a verse and talk about what it means to you. More people are likely to engage and listen if you get their attention in the first few seconds of your video.

"Hi, I'm so-and-so, pastor of First Baptist such-and-such." While identifying yourself is sometimes necessary, don't start with this. Start with your main idea, your power statement, your thesis. Then you can identify yourself and unpack your idea. Don't use two hundred words when twenty will do. This is harder than it seems, especially at first. But if you start thinking this way, it will influence other communications that you do as well. If you're the pastor, your sermons will take on a different rhythm. You may think that the first ten minutes of your sermon are building to the big reveal of your main point, but often the first ten seconds is the time of highest engagement for your listeners.

Boosting Posts

Some posts need promotion to reach a wider audience, such as an invitation to a community event hosted by the church or maybe just a good snippet from a sermon or musical performance that might speak well on its own without context. Remember to link to your full worship services in your posts so that those who want to know more may easily find them without having to navigate your website or Facebook page. Once these particular posts are selected, the Facebook page administrator may "boost" the post by paying to turn it into a "Sponsored" ad. Selecting this option allows you to target a specific demographic (retired men for the sportsman's banquet, etc.).

A good way to use this feature is to keep it "short and sweet" for any promotional materials you boost. Keep videos around thirty seconds, and get to the point in the first sentence. Also, put anything people need to know in the video thumbnail. You can use the "Learn More" button option with the post to drive traffic to your website for more details.

Frequency, Consistency, and Creativity

There is a debate about the pros and cons of posting any content regularly on Facebook. On the one hand, you want your "followers" to count on you for posting material regularly, but posting at the exact same time each week for anything other than a Sunday worship service runs the risk of becoming a stale habit instead of an outlet for innovation. In summer 2020, I began making weekly devotional videos with music, Scripture, and a devotional thought. The series was called "Reflections," and the words "Re-center. Refocus. Reflect." at the beginning of the video invited people to participate. The initial response was enthusiastic, with members liking, commenting, and sharing the videos that occasionally got over two hundred views on Facebook. However, as the pandemic wore on and fatigue began to set in, people stopped liking, sharing, and commenting. The idea had either run its course, or it was time for a reboot.

Incorporating video for worship or other means gives you some tangible data (numbers of views, average watch time, etc.) with which to analyze what you are trying to accomplish. It is important to keep in mind that outside factors also affect what people watch and/or respond to. Posting a reflection on a hymn during a big televised sporting event might not receive the attention commensurate with the efforts you put into making it, but that doesn't necessarily mean you didn't make a good video. Furthermore, consider the culture of your community. What are they used to? If they have always done a weekly Bible study on Wednesday, rain or shine, then posting regularly can continue this aspect of their church culture, even if you record a Zoom session and post it to Facebook. In my particular context, the midweek aspect of our church culture had fizzled out before I arrived, and attempts to revive it were largely futile. My pandemic "Reflections" series lasted three months until I determined that interest in the concept had run its course (only two or three people would click the link that I sent out in weekly emails, though more would view on Facebook). [100] There comes a point when ideas become stale if you simply repeat the same pattern every week. Examine your context to determine the best course of action and regularity when it comes to online posts other than the regular weekly worship service.

CHAPTER 10

THE HYBRID CHURCH

The pandemic of 2020 forced all of us into innovation mode for a short time, and in some places there was great pressure either to continue online or to return to in-person worship in the building. Some churches had members from both extremes threatening to leave the church if the church leadership didn't go along with their side. But one thing was proven true: churches of almost any size are capable of creating online worship events. What does this mean for the future? I'm no prophet, but I sense that some sort of hybrid model will be adopted in order to maintain community in our modern digital world.

The danger of trying to do both is that a church might wind up doing neither well. Larger churches with a full staff might be able to produce an online-only worship on Thursday while also holding in-person worship on Sunday, but this is nearly impossible for a small church to sustain.

In order to find the best hybrid model to fit your context, assess your resources and determine what is sustainable and "worth the effort." Livestreaming your worship service to Facebook from a cell phone may be all that is necessary on a weekly basis to maintain your online presence. But "do not quench the spirit."[101] Let your creativity flow from a sense of mission and outreach rather than obligation. You don't have to post a weekly blog, a meme, a discussion question, a catchy photograph, or a fancy music video every single week at the same time each week. This quickly stifles creativity and becomes a chore and a burden. Instead, as you are inspired, pass it on. You will have some weeks when you are finding and sharing inspiration all the time and other weeks when you won't say anything at all. But keep in mind two things: if you wait until you get it exactly right before you start, you'll never start; and if you post on a fixed schedule, you've prioritized time over content. Just aim to be consistent in how your content enhances the worship event.

Utilizing Zoom

The Zoom application is not just for small groups and deacons' meetings. It is the master tool for the hybrid church. There are many reasons why someone might not be able to be physically present at your meeting, so Zoom (or other video-conferencing software) allows them to connect wherever they are. My church has had members move out of state but still attend book studies via Zoom. One member had a work meeting run late, so she joined our Bible study on Zoom in the car on the ride home. Let's say someone is sick or has company or can't find a babysitter. Now they can join your meeting and at least listen in even if they aren't able to fully engage in the conversation (they need only turn off their microphone and camera). If you have any kind of interactive meeting, simply place a Zoom device near the main speaker, and now anyone in the world can join. Here are some more detailed ideas for putting Zoom to work in your hybrid church:

- *Greeter.* Select a weekly online "greeter" who opens the church's Zoom meeting on a cell phone and moves throughout the building with the camera, allowing the viewers to feel physically present. This technique helps out-of-town or homebound members interact with the community rather than just passively viewing content.
- *Sunday School.* Get a tripod and set up a Zoom device in the actual Sunday school room. If you have multiple classes, you can have multiple Zoom accounts or use other video conference apps like Facebook Messenger or FaceTime.
- *Bible Study.* Open a Zoom session for your Wednesday night Bible study and set the computer or smartphone/tablet next to the presenter so people can interact remotely.
- *Guest Speakers.* Zoom allows guest speakers to present remotely, so you can enlist outside speakers without unnecessary travel expenses. We've had presenters sharing stories, slides, and images with us while they are on location in Africa and we are in our living rooms! Even if your large group prefers meeting in person, simply set up the church Zoom computer on the projector or TV, and participants can gather around it in person or join from home. In the absence of a weekly gathering, my church adopted this model, calling special guest speakers monthly from across the country. We were able to have attendance three to four times what it would be on a weekly frequency. Figure out what best fits your context.

• *Small Groups.* Zoom is ideal for small groups in a busy society where people are overcommitted. It's much easier to log on for thirty minutes than to drive across town. A hybrid approach works well as no projector or TV is needed if a small group gathers in person around a laptop where those not physically present can also join.

• *Other Groups.* Book clubs, breakfast clubs, lunch clubs, college groups, or other affinity groups (which gather people by common interests, occupation, etc.) are all more possible because of technology like Zoom. People may have become "Zoomed out" in the midst of pandemic fatigue, but at least they have learned to use the tool, making it easier to connect in the future.

Philosophy of Adaptation

Let me tell you about a man I'll call Larry. Larry is ninety-five years old and helped build our church. I can't remember a Sunday when Larry did not attend, even after he moved to an assisted living facility. When the pandemic happened, we went immediately to services on Facebook Live, but Larry is almost blind, so he couldn't navigate an iPad. Undeterred, Larry's daughter would call him on Sundays, and he would listen to the audio from the church service over the phone while it played over her phone's speakers. The problem was that he couldn't hear well, so I did some research and found a service that, for a monthly fee, would allow me to upload an audio file of the church service to a 1-800 number that Larry could program into his phone on speed dial. Larry still hasn't missed a service.

Our pastor wrote a book, and we did a small group book study on Zoom. Larry wanted to join but couldn't see to read and there was no audiobook yet. So I recorded myself reading to him, burned it to a CD, and delivered it to the assisted living facility. How did he join the Zoom meetings? His daughter would call into Zoom using her cell phone, and then she would call her father and merge the call so that we could hear both of them. Larry didn't miss a meeting, even though he hasn't left his room in ten months.

Do you see the potential here?

My mom plays an online Scrabble-type game called Words with Friends with a stranger in New York, and they've become friends even though they've never met. She shared with this friend a link to our Sunday services. Neither my mom nor her friend from New York are church members, but they both rarely miss a service.

Do you see the potential here?

We had a couple join the church *online. During the pandemic.* They moved to the area and found our worship services on our website.

Do you see the potential here?

We filmed our Keyboards at Christmas concert for a virtual-only presentation this year. When it happened live, we usually had maybe 100 people in the room. As mentioned earlier, the YouTube video has been viewed over 3,500 times.

Do you see the potential here?

Families are going to go on vacation. Now they can stay connected out of town. Church members are going to get the flu. Now they can worship at home without feeling obligated to come to the church building before they have fully recovered. Sometimes people have a horrible week and need to sleep in on Sunday. They can catch up with the service later.

There are downsides to online church. Some people don't want to volunteer to read Scripture during the service if they know they will appear on Facebook Live. Some people will get out of the habit of coming to church altogether. But those challenges are going to occur anyway, and in my opinion, the benefits outweigh the risks.

Let's talk about the learning curve. With a full staff and a robust budget, large churches have been playing this online game for years. But now technology has finally become accessible for the small church to go online and to do it well. However, it's important to strike a balance and only do what enhances your current offerings without staff burnout. Even with a robust budget, it is difficult if not impossible to compete with the front-runners in online or television ministry in terms of production quality, so it's important to remember that the best you can do is the best you can do.

Reflection: The Ethics of Worship

What good is worship? What is good worship? It's funny how the order of the words changes the meaning of the question. But the idea is the same: what is "good" and what is "worship" are connected. Or at least they should be.

All across America there are church signs emblazoned with the words "Worship Service" along with the times and a few other bits of information. We pass them every day as we travel through the city or the country, sometimes multiple churches just on the way to the grocery store. But has it ever struck you how those two words belong together? Somehow, through the ages worship became what you do at the end of the week to get right with God after all that you've done wrong during the week. There's nothing wrong with that. But isn't there more to it? Maybe that way of looking at things is backwards. Maybe a worship service is a call to worship *service*, to a life aimed at loving God and making this world more like God's kingdom. If you look at it this way, worship is not just a Sunday morning ritual to make you feel better. Worship is a way of life.

As noted earlier, the word "worship" comes from the Old English for "worth ship," meaning that you are conveying "worth," or value, to something—in this case to God. In Spanish, there's a connection to "adoration." But how does one go about adoring and "worthing" something? I think there's a connection with how we live, and it helps to look at some other languages. We get our word "liturgy" from the Greek for "work" and "people," an act performed to benefit the community. The German word for worship puts together "God" and "service"—again defined as something done for others, not just a meeting with songs and a sermon. Other words for worship in Spanish, French, and Italian are connected to the cultivation of the earth and, by extension, the nurturing of faith, community, and relationship with God.[102]

We turn up our noses at Old Testament notions of sacrifice as "offerings," but that was the people's act of worship. And even in that ritual, we see a connection to service. Isaiah calls the people out, as if God is saying, "What to me is the multitude of your sacrifices? . . . I have had enough of burnt offerings. . . . I do not delight in the blood . . . cease to do evil, learn to do good; seek justice, rescue the oppressed, defend the orphan, plead for the widow" (Isa 1:11-17, NRSV). What would the world look like if we saw our "offering" to God as this list of actions?

So what is good worship? It's offering service. It's something that calls us to praise God through serving other human beings. What good is worship? It's transformation. It's something that calls us to change the way we see God, ourselves, and our neighbors. We are called to be God's people—not just on Sunday but always.

CHAPTER 11

IDEAS FOR VIDEO WORSHIP SEGMENTS (ONLINE OR IN PERSON)

This chapter outlines some creative ways to use videos as part of your worship experience, and if you have screens in your sanctuary, you can use these videos in either setting, online or in person. It takes longer to produce a good-quality video segment, but if done well, it can have a stronger impact on those present in worship (we are already comfortable consuming visual media, after all!), and it also gives you the opportunity to share the individual segment on social media, where it might gain a broader audience and spark interest in your church. Be careful to strike a healthy balance and be mindful of your resources. It can be overkill to produce one of these videos every week, and, as one of my choir members would say, "The juice might not be worth the squeeze!" In other words, apply the "less is more" philosophy, and use these tools when you have a special occasion or find a particularly inspirational idea. You can't do a children's drama every Sunday, but you can do one for Christmas, one for Easter, or maybe even one per sermon series or quarterly. Find a balance using the assets and resources you already possess and stay focused on the goal of enhancing worship. You may find yourself invested in a project where the result is not what you had hoped and you don't think it should be viewed. That's OK! Learn from that process and do better next time. You don't have to show a video just because you filmed it.

Screens

The beauty of a hybrid model for worship is that you can use videos in both settings as long as you have a screen in your sanctuary, and if not, it is less invasive and expensive to install one than it used to be. If it will only be used occasionally, a seventy-five-inch television can be seen by almost everyone in a small church, and it can be mounted on a pedestal with wheels and discretely hidden away when not in use. Someone with a laptop in the front row could control the screen with minimal distractions, and at my church, our two TVs are loud enough so that we don't even have to run them to the soundboard. If you plan to use the screen more frequently, then a more permanent arrangement can be made, but this usually involves higher buy-in from a building and grounds committee or other church polity. People are reluctant to change anything about the sanctuary until they see how it can enhance the experience.

Music Ministry

Music is probably equally as important as preaching for your congregation, and hybrid worship affords opportunities to showcase your church's talents to a broader audience with both promotional materials and elements of worship. You could film a small portion of a large choir piece and post it to Facebook as a preview in order to increase engagement and excitement about an upcoming performance and entice potential newcomers to attend. Small ensembles could be prerecorded and inserted as part of the live service. In cases when instrumental music is required (for Communion or other occasions where music is desired to fill the atmosphere), prerecording a piece allows you the chance to hire musicians who might be engaged at other churches on Sunday morning. Furthermore, having recordings of your own musicians gives you material to use when promoting other church events. For example, the previous music minister at our church recorded a full album with the choir, which was much larger during his tenure. This CD became a useful resource during the pandemic, and I've used the audio in various promotional materials, including our welcome page for guests on our website, intro videos for hybrid services, and background music for other short videos.

Using a green screen, an audio interface with a condenser microphone, and a piano track (only for reference when recording; I removed it for the final product), I created a cappella versions of hymns using a quartet made up of my strongest singers (https://youtu.be/zo0S8ymJyf4). During the pandemic when we weren't hosting in-person services, these hymns served as integral parts of worship, bringing new life to hymns with rich harmonies and a renewed focus on the lyrics as well as the faces of the performers. I mixed the audio myself using Apple's GarageBand, blending the voices and adding a sense of space with reverb, compression, limiters, and equalization (see tutorial at SensingGodOnline.com). For the video, I clipped a $40 green screen to a bookshelf in my office, and I filmed each singer individually with earbuds so they could hear the piano and stay in sync with one another.

Heritage Fellowship worship quartet singing a cappella hymns. These were recorded (each singer individually) in my church office with a piece of green fabric clipped to the bookshelf behind them and a ring light with cell phone holder to film. I captured audio from the automated piano on the website SongSelect, importing it into GarageBand. Using the Focusrite iTrack Solo audio interface, the singers would listen to the piano track as they sang, and for the final video, I deleted the piano track and processed the audio using GarageBand's limiter, compressor, equalization, and reverb.

One way to enhance music for hybrid services is to incorporate visual elements that coincide with the lyrics. A hymn like "For the Beauty of the Earth" could be enhanced by showing video or still images of landscapes. If you have a screen in the sanctuary, these images could be displayed during the song. Software programs like PowerPoint allow you to put text over the images, and ones like ProPresenter allow you to put text over videos. This can be useful for displaying lyrics. If there are no screens in the sanctuary, using a tool like Switcher Studio would allow you to display the images for viewers at home, giving them a more reflective experience.

Drama and Scripture

We've all witnessed a live performance of a homemade skit that made us cringe more than it enhanced the worship service. These elements can be used with more control if they are prerecorded. Children can be enlisted to read a verse, and they might not be as nervous or as likely to freeze in front of the crowd if they can film it beforehand. Plus, they could do several takes, allowing you to choose the best one.

Youth Ministry

Youth are often natural, intuitive users and consumers of digital media, but that easy media use doesn't always translate into a sense of "connectedness." If they did something clumsy or "stupid" at school, and someone captured it or the aftermath on video, they must now suffer ridicule for days until the mob moves on to someone else. Youth need coaching and direction on healthy practices for social media, and they crave (even if subconsciously) authentic connection with their family and friends.

One way to foster connection is with occasional family gatherings with guided experiences and interactions. During the first phase of the 2020 pandemic, one church in Raleigh facilitated a seder meal (a Jewish meal commemorating the exodus from Egypt) for youth and their families during Lent.[103] They sent out a list of required materials and possible substitutions, encouraging participants to "do the best you can" to assemble the elements of the symbolic meal. The beauty of this event was that the whole family could work together around the kitchen table but still be in community with the larger church group via Zoom. The youth minister suggests that if each family had participated in isolation, teenagers might have viewed it as "lame," but because it was something the entire group could do together (though apart), it at least felt "less lame."

Depending on your church culture, events like this could be difficult to do regularly, but if done well and with large buy-in—that is, participation and interest—from families, they can quickly become meaningful traditions in your community. The Maundy Thursday seder meal could become a coveted tradition for your entire church, ministering to people at every age demographic and even pulling in the grandparents. Other special events could be assembling a family Advent wreath, passing the baton at graduation, honoring Ash Wednesday, "blessing" the journey to summer camp, etc.

Children's Ministry

For children, engaging physical participation is natural and even expected. During the 2020 pandemic, Sunday school teachers came to me to figure out a plan to get materials to students. We managed to film the lessons early in the week and mail out paper copies of handouts and other materials to our small group of children. In post-pandemic life, this might be a logistical challenge, but with a few creative, enthusiastic educators on your team, you can design occasional videos that guide children or even their entire family through an activity that brings a biblical story or church tradition to life. Even simple suggestions can generate a meaningful experience that engages the entire family. For example, you might post this to the church Facebook page: "Pick flowers with your family and talk about the Easter story. Take a group selfie and post it to our page." Depending on your demographic and human resources at your church, you might even have each family submit video clips of what they've learned through the experience, which can then be edited for use as part of a worship service.

Sermons

There will always be times when it is not possible for people to meet for worship in the building: inclement weather, other health concerns (the pastor has the flu), etc. Having a plan and infrastructure in place to film a sermon at home can remove the strain from other resources. Pastors who are accustomed to preaching more than one sermon per week for multiple services may even wish to create a separate sermon especially produced for online viewing. Regardless of the circumstances, here are some suggestions for filming a sermon from home:

• *Tripod.* Keep a tripod and ring light in your home for last-minute use as necessary. These can be obtained from Amazon for less than $50, and they make it easier to produce a quality video using only a cell phone. (If you plan to use these at your church office too, either purchase two of each item or keep your set in the car so you'll have them available in either location.)

• *Framing the Shot.* Position the cell phone camera as close to you as possible in order to get the best audio, and keep the "rule of thirds" in mind when framing the shot. You want your torso to fill most of the frame either dead centered or slightly off to one side. Imagine three grid lines on your screen both horizontally and vertically, and center yourself in the shot or positioned either left or right of where the center lines intersect.

• *Distractions.* Make the background as free of distractions as possible, in both audio and visuals. Pay attention to the other sounds around you. A leaf blower outside might not seem that distracting while you're preaching, but it can take viewers' minds off the subject. If you can, place your chair near a wall with a clean, organized view behind you. Bookshelves are nice if they're not too "busy." A blank wall is OK, but a tidy living space is more inviting. If you can afford to keep a foldable green screen at home (less than $50) and have time to edit, then utilize the "bokeh effect" by taking a still picture and blurring it slightly in order to create a sense of depth. This photo could be of a setting at your church, somewhere outdoors, or literally anywhere in the world. Just make it relevant, and avoid backgrounds that can be too distracting.

CHAPTER 12

EQUIPPING A CONGREGATION FOR DIGITAL LITERACY

Many church members are newcomers to the digital world, and they need extra help navigating this new space. There is some irony in that we have had the technology for years now to reach our homebound members with the Sunday message, but we haven't taken time to learn how to use the tools available to us, and they likely would not feel comfortable accessing the material without some help. This chapter explores the last piece of the puzzle to online worship—equipping members who are not tech savvy with the skills they need to access worship online without the burden and frustration of confusion or the embarrassment of failure. In some cases, a bad experience of trying and failing to get connected during the pandemic might work against you for future ventures.

Confidence

Perhaps the greatest challenge (and irony) is that the people who most need this technologically connected worship experience are members of the older generation who are least likely to learn the skills necessary to access the material. As a rule, it's generally easier to raise money to buy them Wi-Fi and iPads than to persuade them to use such tools if they are not already tech savvy. However, this trend will decline in future years as more and more generations leave the workforce and enter retirement having used similar technology in their careers. In other words, lay the groundwork now, and more people will make use of it as time goes on. Your goal should be to build confidence in your congregation to use at least one piece of technology without fear or frustration. It takes patience to lead them down this road, but you will all be stronger on the other side.

IT Office Hours or "Hotline"

Right now, you can think of someone in your church who is great with technology, and hopefully they are on staff or volunteer regularly. If you can enlist their help to make themselves available, they can be a great community resource that helps members stay connected online and develop digital literacy in your community. Think about how access to technology could improve the quality of life of homebound people who have never had a video chat with their out-of-state children, grandchildren, or other relatives. It can be difficult to determine who needs help, but making the effort to provide this service to your congregation can offer a point of connection and ministry opportunities that might not otherwise occur. Often people are unaware of what questions to ask, so it is important to coach whoever is tasked with the role of IT assistant to be aware of a variety of skill levels and to answer even rudimentary questions with grace.

Smart TVs

If your worship services are on YouTube, they can be easily accessed via the YouTube app on a smart TV. For members with standard TVs, you could host a "get connected" drive where people donate $40 Roku devices that will connect to any TV with an HDMI input, and they allow the installation of the YouTube app. A knowledgeable staff member or volunteer would need to be available to train the church member in the use of the device and to create a YouTube account for them that is subscribed to your church's channel for easy access on the TV. This challenge is compounded if there is no current Wi-Fi at that particular member's house, but if they are willing to learn, there is probably someone willing to donate money to help them get connected, and this can be part of your "get connected" drive.

Smartphones and Tablets

Smartphones and tablets have become more affordable in recent years, with iPads starting at less than $350 and iPod Touches or other smartphones or similar devices starting at less than $200. Because many people like to upgrade when newer models are released, you have an opportunity to "recycle" old devices. You could provide a place at your church for people to donate their old devices (with personal info erased), which could then be redistributed to those who need one. You may need to designate someone to help people erase data from their old devices, and that same IT point person can also help new users create accounts and learn how to use the device. Small suggestions can help someone in isolation become more proficient at staying connected. Once when visiting a church member, I saw her power her iPad down completely after showing me a picture. I asked her about this, and she said, "Well, that's how you turn it off, right?" She had no idea that these devices could simply be put to sleep, and my simple tip saved her minutes of frustration waiting on the device to power down and back on again later. It takes vulnerability to accept advice, but it can be better received if it is delivered with humility, patience, and understanding—all pastoral traits to be developed!

Computers

Someone in your congregation might be savvier on a computer than a tablet or smartphone, but they may not have access to the updated models due to a lack of resources or even the attitude of "the old computer still works, so why would I buy a new one?" They may not realize how quickly technology becomes obsolete or how greatly improved a current $250 laptop can be versus a $2,500 desktop from years ago. This is where education comes in handy, and there may be someone in your church willing to donate machines to have on hand for those who would like to be connected. You might start a "Connections Ministry" to help members at every age stay connected and up to date with everything going on in your community.

Small Groups

Book clubs, Sunday school classes, accountability groups, etc. can be offered with a hybrid or entirely online option as long as you have a motivated group willing to put in the effort to meet regularly. All it takes is equipping a tech-savvy member of the group with coaching and training on how to take the meetings online with Zoom or FaceTime in order to make the group available to anyone who can't be there in person.

CHAPTER 13

BEYOND WORSHIP— MARKETING AND OTHER CONSIDERATIONS

Once you have a body of video services to work with, the possibilities are endless for how you can put this material to use. Remember that the digital world we inhabit is oversaturated with content, so it's up to you to find ways to get your message across in attention-grabbing, short-form ways. A marketing consultant or team of staff members can certainly help, but you can learn ways to do this on your own. What is *the* most important sentence from the sermon? Make a post with a video clip of your saying it or a find a related image and put that text over it. If it's powerful enough and captures enough attention, your members will share it on social media, and you won't have to spend a dime on advertising. Their friends will see it and perhaps click on your church's page to learn more. This marketing strategy follows current trends of very large churches in the Atlanta area, and if you have videos of your services, you already have the master files available (i.e., your Sunday messages or services) to create multiple pieces of content. Here are some more detailed ideas:

• *Memes.* A staff member or volunteer can identify the best quote (or the pastor might suggest the "heart of the message") and make a meme (a picture with a quote) that can be posted to the church Facebook page.

• *Showcase Video.* Special musical numbers or key moments from the sermon may be posted as separate short videos. Church seekers and current members are more likely to view three minutes rather than thirty, and this brief content is more easily digested by a wider audience. Members will share these "sermon replays," increasing the name recognition of your church in the community and spreading your message far beyond your walls. The goal might not be to go viral, but this has been known to happen if the content is especially memorable.

• *Ads in Local Print Media.* You might already publish church information in a local newspaper or magazine. Be sure to list your church website on anything you promote in print. More importantly, make the website as user-friendly as possible for a first-time visitor. (See below.)

• *Web Design.* I enlisted the help of a marketing professional to review our church website. I spent several days working with her, drafting and editing a narrative that explained the nuances of our community identity, and I finally posted my writing to our website, sending the link to the marketing professional for one final proofread. The entire process was eye-opening and valuable, but she gave me perhaps the best piece of advice in our final phone call. "Justin, it looks great, but what time is your service?" In all my attention to detail, I had neglected to provide the most obvious piece of information that someone would need in order to attend our church.

Once you have been swimming in a community culture for any length of time, it can become difficult to see the water. This is why it's important to enlist the help of outsiders, friends or acquaintances who can offer a fresh perspective on your information and its digital presentation. If your budget allows you to hire a professional, heed their advice. But even after you think it's finalized, show it to a friend who doesn't attend your church. You'll be surprised at the advice they might offer or what they might notice that you have overlooked. You might discover a cover image with a background that makes it look like you have a cross blooming out of your head, or there may be a glaring typo in one of your headlines. Or maybe you have opted for the "fire hose" approach and included too much information instead of a smooth, flowing stream of information that is more easily digested. First impressions are everything, and you have about *three seconds* to make an impression on someone once they go to your web page (a general web search of "three-second rule" will lead you to numerous articles about this phenomenon).

• *High-quality Images.* Never underestimate the power of images. You can communicate lots of information about your church without writing a single word. For example, below is the first photo on the scrolling photo gallery on our church's homepage. It might not be the best photograph in the world, but it conveys a wealth of information. During the marketing research process, members identified our traditional worship services and music as one of their favorite characteristics of our church. From this photograph, newcomers to our website can tell within a few seconds, even if at a subconscious level, the following information:

* This church sings classic, familiar hymns.

* They use a piano.

* They have a traditional choir—a small one that might be open for new members to easily join.

* People dress formally for these services.

This is the first image on my church's homepage (heritagecanton.com), and it is designed to convey as much information as possible within the first few seconds of viewing the web page. Potential new members can quickly determine worship style and preferred dress code from this image, two key factors that play into people's decisions about which church to attend.

It's important to recognize that not everyone knows how to use every platform, and different generations gravitate toward different media. When I was a high school English teacher, almost no student had a Facebook account, but they would incessantly engage with Snapchat throughout their waking hours. Facebook seems to engage the older audiences more, while Instagram and Twitter are somewhere in between. These trends will come and go, but it is important to know the demographic trends and who is using which platform in order to engage them more effectively.

The youth minister might make memes and short videos to send to the youth group via Snapchat while the senior adult minister makes Facebook posts and emails a weekly newsletter. If you are the only paid staff, volunteers can be coached and trained in how to accomplish these goals, or there are several ways to link accounts and post one thing to multiple platforms at once (which some video hosting services offer for a price).

You can't suddenly be the mega-church pastor rolling out brilliance at every turn. But you can find your niche and make the most of what you have.

Your "Brand"

Whether you are aware of it or not, your church has a "brand" or a public image that exists independently of you as a church leader. This is something that can be shaped by your leadership, planning, and online presence. If you can pay a graphic designer to design a logo, this can easily be included in your video worship services, your website, your social media posts, and any print media you may purchase. Put a good logo everywhere, and people will suddenly start to associate you with something. If your staff or deacons or other leadership can agree on "the most important thing" to communicate about your church, then people will start to associate you with it.

Our church only has about one hundred members, but we regularly host a local nonprofit project called the MUST Ministries "Summer Lunch" program, which hand-delivers meals to low-income students throughout the community. This ministry is prominent on our website and in print media, and volunteers talk about the program as they are helping complete tasks like buying groceries, making sandwiches, packing bags, or delivering the meals. People hear "Heritage Fellowship," and they immediately think, "Oh, you're the church that hands out the lunch bags!" This makes a statement about our values as a community, and perfect strangers are willing to donate to our cause while we stand in line at Walmart with overflowing shopping carts filled with food.

What do you wish to be known for? Identify it, and then pour a majority of your resources into doing that one thing to the best of your abilities. It helps if this is already something your church is doing or has been doing for years. Problems arise if church leadership has a different idea of the "one thing" for which you wish to be known, and any change to the status quo requires a strong and healthy buy-in from your community. Prior to my church's "Summer Lunch" program, their primary fundraiser and project for community outreach was a "Holiday Bazaar" where community members would donate or make a variety of goods to be auctioned and sold in the fellowship hall. This cost the church little in terms of spending church funds, and it earned an extra $10,000–$15,000 to finance other mission projects throughout the year. But the cost in human resources was high. Everyone had to pitch in. Failing health caused many members to take a back seat for the bazaar, and there seemed to be no one to take their place. The pastor at the time sensed a need for change and presented the "Summer Lunch" idea as a replacement. Change is always hard, but once people began to see the impact of this new project and how it was easier for volunteers to participate, the change was successfully made.

A colleague of mine worked for a church plant in Atlanta that would see thirty attendees for Sunday worship at a local school cafeteria. Attendance at worship was small, but this community valued families and education, so they hosted school supply drives, block parties, and other family-oriented events in their neighborhood. Hundreds attended these events, and scores of people would volunteer to help. His church became known for these family events, and soon the online services saw hundreds of views. If you can rally around a cause, your community might participate even if they don't officially join your church, and if they are connected with your cause, they are more likely to have a look at your worship and Sunday messages. Your impact in the community could increase even if your membership remains the same.

CHAPTER 14

CONCLUSION— "BE THE CHURCH"

Reflections on Life in In-between Times

At the time of this writing, the intensity of the pandemic has eased with the growing prevalence of vaccines in the Unites States, but so far only hints of "normal" have returned. We've been living between times. It's happened before, but we didn't stay there long. And why would we want to? It's the tension between what is and what should be that we can't abide. We need to know. We need certainty. Maybe that's why the TV preachers are so popular—all that certainty. But during the COVID-19 pandemic, nothing has been certain. Every time we take one timid step back toward normal, the debates begin again.

It turns out there's a term for what we have experienced, and this isn't the first time it's happened, nor will it be the last. In English, we struggle with the concept in everyday usage, but our Spanish-speaking friends might find it easier to grasp because their word for "hoping" and their word for "waiting" is the same: *esperando*. One starts from a place of dread, and the other begins with anticipation. But they've always been a little mixed up. Maybe the word "longing" better illustrates this tension, but many have called it liminal space, or, as Fr. Richard Rohr writes,

> an inner state and sometimes an outer situation where we can begin to think and act in new ways. It is where we are betwixt and between, having left one room or stage of life but not yet entered the next. We usually enter liminal space when our former way of being is challenged or changed—perhaps when we lose a job or a loved one, during illness, at the birth of a child, or a major relocation. It is a graced time, but often does not feel "graced" in any way. In such space, we are not certain or in

control. This global pandemic we now face is an example of an immense, collective liminal space.[104]

In this in-between space, our spiritual senses become at once more acute and more unbearable. Many turn to unhealthy coping mechanisms to get through. But Fr. Rohr goes on to suggest,

> In liminal space we sometimes need to not-do and not-perform according to our usual successful patterns. We actually need to fail abruptly and deliberately falter to understand other dimensions of life. We need to be silent instead of speaking, experience emptiness instead of fullness, anonymity instead of persona, and pennilessness instead of plenty. In liminal space, we descend and intentionally do not come back out or up immediately. It takes time but this experience can help us reenter the world with freedom and new, creative approaches to life.

We need to surrender. We can't change our immediate circumstances, but we can be changed by them. Maybe if we step into the silence instead of doing everything we can to run back toward "normal," the true light will start to come into focus.

The first converts to "the Way" of Jesus were in such a liminal space after the crucifixion. There was no centralized (or even easily recognized) church. There was no New Testament. There was no normal. Jesus had turned it all upside down. The new converts knew "longing" perhaps better than us. Even after the resurrection, I'm sure they would have given anything to go back to walking with Jesus and following his lead instead of having to figure out everything for themselves. So what did they do to navigate the "in-between" time? Acts 2:42 says, "They devoted themselves to the apostles' teaching and fellowship, to the breaking of bread and the prayers" (NRSV).

Then the situation gets political in an unexpected way in verses 44-45: "All who believed were together and had all things in common; they would sell their possessions and goods and distribute the proceeds to all, as any had need." Were they Communists? Is this Socialism? Is this an overstatement? An exaggeration? I have no idea. And that's not what matters. The important thing is that they helped each other carry the load through a difficult time, and we should follow their lead. The world needs us right now. The church might not be able to meet exactly the same way it did before the pandemic, but we can meet the needs of our neighbors.

In the 1950s my grandfather broke his leg badly. He was a logger in the North Carolina mountains, and a tree kicked back on him. When my dad looked up at the sound of a scream, he saw the leg at a right angle to where it should have been. And that should have been the end of my grandfather's prospects. There was no unemployment or health insurance or food banks. There was no stimulus check coming in the mail. There was nothing standing between him and hunger and homelessness. That's when the neighbors started showing up. They didn't say much. They just took his logging truck and equipment and went to work. Each day someone different came and did all the work and gave my grandfather all the money. It just took a day's sacrifice for each of them, but it saved my grandfather and his family. If enough people pitch in and do something in times of crisis, it can change everything.

We've got to put aside our partisanship and opinions. We've got to step into the silence instead of running back to "normal." We don't need to go back. We need to get better. When the waiting world is hungry, hope hands them a box of food. We don't have to say anything. We're all in this together; if we share our resources now as the disciples did back then, we can make it through this "in-between" time and come out better on the other side. I'm waiting and hoping and longing for nothing else right now.

Consider for a moment the history of the Christian church and its ability to adapt and navigate an ever-changing set of contexts and societal demands. How the church gathers for worship has been aided by ancillary activities that are of paramount significance to the overall mission of the church. This seems to suggest that what you do outside the church walls is equally if not more important than what goes on in the sanctuary. Paul's "living sacrifice" analogy in Romans 12 extends worship to include the very lives we lead. To remain relevant and present in the twenty-first century and adapt to its digital demands, the church must now employ the digital means available to host and promote worship experiences online.

The church has never been about the building. It's ironic that we spend so much time trying to get people to come to church. What if we focused more on *being the church* wherever we are right now?

When the pandemic of 2020 started, many of us felt that the isolation from our church family and attendance at online worship was "not so bad." But that was a short-lived perspective. The novelty wore off. Some of the fear subsided. Some of the fear got worse. What began as a distant, far-off news report soon landed close to home as we began to know someone who contracted (or even died of!) the virus, someone who lost a job, or someone who simply could not cope with the new reality. Or maybe we are one of those people.

Now is the time when the world needs the church more than ever, and it has nothing to do with higher Sunday school attendance or a capital campaign or what color to paint the new fellowship hall. In an email, my friend reminded me of a common sermon illustration: the most important symbol in the church building is not the cross or the altar or any of that but the sign at the back of the church saying EXIT in glowing red. That's what everything that happens in the church is for. The problem is that now we can't even go back inside the building . . . but maybe that's a good thing, at least for now. It's forcing us to rethink what it means to be the church in the world.

For far too long, we've relied on others to do the work of the church. Depending on our unique skill sets and talents, we've let others sing in the choir or play the piano. We've let others teach Sunday school or do the preaching. But those are just things that happen inside the church. What about outside? Well, the same is true. We've let others go on mission trips or go visit a sick friend. We've let others staff the soup kitchen or hand out clean socks to the homeless. But those activities are obviously connected to the church.

What about just being the church wherever we are? What would that look like? I think we've been missing the point for a long time. Jesus didn't talk about which banners to hang according to the Christian calendar or which sound system to buy and how to hang the speakers so they're not distracting during worship. Jesus didn't talk about which hymn fit which passage of Scripture or how the music sounded or made anyone feel. Jesus didn't recommend which Sunday school material to use or how to make a casserole that would feed thirty-eight people. Not that any of those things are unimportant, but they're not the most important parts of being the church.

Jesus talked a lot about *being*. Being a good neighbor. Being of the right heart and mind. Being kind and compassionate. Having lived through the pandemic when we couldn't be in the church building, we finally have a chance to be the church that we've been missing all along.

People are still struggling all around us. Be the church to them. Find out what they need and help them or find someone who can. No, you can't go see them. But you can call them. You can write them a card. You can order food and have it delivered to them. You can order toilet paper wholesale and put a box with a "Free" sign on it out by the road. You can pay a light bill. You can donate to a food bank. You can get over that grudge you've been holding. You can be kind. You can be compassionate. You can be patient. You can be love. This is your act of worship.

God is love, and you are never more like God than when you are loving your neighbor. And so what if you can't see them? We can't see God, but that doesn't make God any less real. Your neighbors are real, and their needs are real too.

You can't change the way the world is right now, but you can change something.

How are we going to look at this time? As forced isolation that we can do nothing about? Or as a chance to rethink who we are?

We have been given a gift—a chance to be the church again, wherever we are. We've been deployed.

The "ends of the earth" are now only a Wi-Fi signal away, and to stay out of the game is to let the televangelists dominate the market and provide the singular vision of what it means to follow Christ. There is a rich, healthy diversity within Christianity, and making your message and worship available online enriches that diversity and enhances the potential for the world to encounter the presence of God. Navigating the world of digital worship is not for the faint of heart, nor is it without risks. But it is worth it. God, the omnipresent, has been online from the beginning, but people need your help to sense that presence.

BIBLIOGRAPHY

Abram, David. *The Spell of the Sensuous: Perception and Language in a More-Than-Human World.* New York: Vintage Books, 1996.

Ackerman, Diane. *A Natural History of the Senses.* New York: Vintage Books, 1990.

Aquinas, St. Thomas. *Summa Theologiae: A Concise Translation,* edited by Timothy McDermott. Allen, TX: Christian Classics, 1989.

Ashlin-Mayo, Bryce. *Digital Mission: A Practical Guide for Ministry Online.* Toronto: Tyndale Academic Press, 2020. Kindle edition.

Baum, Jacob M. *Reformation of the Senses.* Studies in Sensory History. Springfield, University of Illinois Press, 2019. Kindle edition.

Bechtel, Carol M. *Touching the Altar: The Old Testament for Christian Worship.* Grand Rapids: Eerdmans, 2008. Kindle edition.

Bedford, Nancy Elizabeth. 2012. "The Beauty of God: The Senses, Liturgy, and Christian Discipleship." *Journal of Latin American Theology* 7/2: 37–59.

Berger, Peter L. *The Many Altars of Modernity: Toward a Paradigm for Religion in a Pluralist Age.* Boston: Walter de Gruyter, Inc., 2014.

Bevins, Winfield. *Ever Ancient, Ever New: The Allure of Liturgy for a New Generation.* Grand Rapids: Zondervan, 2019.

Billy Graham Evangelistic Association. "A Look Back at Billy Graham's Largest Ever Crusade." *Billy Graham,* June 3, 2019. billygraham. org/story/seoul-south-korea-a-look-back-at-billy-grahams-largest-ever-crusade/.

Borchert, Gerald L. "The Lord of Form and Freedom: A New Testament Perspective on Worship." *Review & Expositor* 80/1 (Winter 1983): 5–18.

Boulton, Matthew Myer. *God Against Religion: Rethinking Christian Theology through Worship* Grand Rapids: Eerdmans, 2008. Kindle edition.

Burkhart, John E., *Worship: A Searching Examination of the Liturgical Experience.* Philadelphia: Westminster Press, 1982. Quoted in Duck, *Worship for the Whole People of God.*

Candler, Peter M., Jr. *Theology, Rhetoric, Manuduction, or Reading Scripture Together on the Path to God.* Grand Rapids: Eerdmans, 2006.

Caputo, John D. *The Weakness of God: A Theology of the Event.* Bloomington, IN: Indiana University Press, 2006.

Carvalhaes, Cláudio. "Making 'Sense' in Theological Education." *ARTS* 25/2 (2014): 27–36.

Cherry, Constance M. *The Worship Architect: A Blueprint for Designing Culturally Relevant and Biblically Faithful Services.* Grand Rapids: Baker Academic, 2010.

Chisham, David. "Latent and Manifest Icons: Exploring Creative and Visual Narratives of Worship at Rockville Christian Church." DMin thesis, Drew University, 2012.

Clarkson, Joel. *Sensing God: Experiencing the Divine in Nature, Food, Music, and Beauty.* NavPress, 2021. Kindle edition.

Cron, Ian Morgan, and Suzanne Stabile. *The Road Back to You: An Enneagram Journey to Self-Discovery.* Illinois: InterVarsity Press, 2016.

Crosby, Fanny. "Blessed Assurance." *Palmer's Guide to Holiness and Revival Miscellany.* July 1873.

Dickens, Charles. *A Tale of Two Cities.* 1859. Barnes & Noble Classics, 2004.

Dix, Dom Gregory. *The Shape of the Liturgy.* London: Bloomsbury, 2005.

Driver, Tom F. *Liberating Rites: Understanding the Transformative Power of Ritual.* Charleston: BookSurge, LLC., 2006.

Duck, Ruth C. *Worship for the Whole People of God: Vital Worship for the 21st Century.* Louisville: Westminster John Knox Press, 2013.

Dyer, Thomas William, Jr. "We Are All Thomas Now: Millennial Christians and the Need for New Theological Worlds at the First Baptist Church of Augusta, Georgia." DMin thesis, Mercer University, 2019.

Eliade, Mircea. *The Sacred & The Profane: The Nature of Religion.* San Diego: Harcourt Brace & Co., 1987.

FitzPatrick, P.J. *In Breaking of Bread: The Eucharist and Ritual.* Cambridge: Cambridge University Press, 1993.

Golliher, Jeff. *A Deeper Faith: A Journey into Spirituality.* New York: Penguin, 2008.

Gordon, Elisabeth. "Using Multiple Senses to Improve Memory." *UNIL Université de Lausanne,* https://wp.unil.ch/discoverunil/2016/11/using-multiple-senses-to-improve-memory/#:~:text=Yet%20the%20neuroscientist%20points%20out,remember%20what%20you've%20learned.

Graham, Elaine L. *Transforming Practice: Pastoral Theology in an Age of Uncertainty.* Eugene, OR: Wipf and Stock Publishers, 1996.

Grimes, Ronald L. *Deeply into the Bone: Re-inventing Rites of Passage.* Berkley: University of California Press, 2000.

Heath, Chip, and Dan Heath. *The Power of Moments: Why Certain Experiences Have Extraordinary Impact.* Simon & Schuster, 2017. Kindle edition.

Hirsh, Sandra Krebs. *Soultypes: Matching Your Personality and Spiritual Path.* Minneapolis: Augsburg Books, 2006.

Jones, W. Paul. *Theological Worlds: Understanding the Alternative Rhythms of Christian Belief.* Nashville: Abingdon Press, 1989.

———. *Worlds Within a Congregation: Dealing with Theological Diversity.* Nashville: Abingdon Press, 2000.

Jungmann, Josef A (Josef Andreas). "The Sense for the Sacred." *Worship* 30/6 (May 1956): 354–60.

King, Shaun. Pastor of Johns Creek Baptist Church. Interview by author, 22 October 2020. Zoom teleconference video recording. Johns Creek Baptist Church, Alpharetta, GA.

Kirk, David R. "When You Come Together: Gathered Worship in the New Testament." *Foundations* (Affinity) 76 (Spr 2019): 34–60.

Lea, Michael S. "The Incarnation of Blessing: How do Worshipers at First Baptist Church of West Jefferson, NC Experience Blessing in the Confluence of the Sermon and Liturgical Response?" DMin thesis, Mercer University, 2017.

Lewis, C. S. *Mere Christianity.* New York: Touchstone, 1943. Quoted in Witvliet, "The Opening of Worship: Trinity."

Loder, James E. *The Transforming Moment.* Colorado Springs: Helmers & Howard, 1989.

Long, Kimberly Bracken. *The Worshiping Body: The Art of Leading Worship.* Louisville: Westminster John Knox Press, 2009.

Maas, Robin, and Gabriel O'Donnell, eds. *Spiritual Traditions for the Contemporary Church.* Nashville: Abingdon Press, 1990.

Martin, Ralph P. "New Testament Worship: Some Puzzling Practices." *Andrews University Seminary Studies* 31/2 (Sum 1993): 119–26.

McHugh, Adam S. *Introverts in the Church: Finding Our Place in an Extroverted Culture.* Downers Grove, IL: InterVarsity Press 2017.

Mitchell, Nathan D. "Reforms, Protestant and Catholic." *The Oxford History of Christian Worship.* Oxford: Oxford University Press, 2006.

———. "Liturgy and Life: Lessons in Benedict." *Worship* 82/2 (2008): 161–74.

Moschella, Mary Clark. *Ethnography as a Pastoral Practice: An Introduction.* Cleveland: The Pilgrim Press, 2008.

Mulholland, M. Robert. *Invitation to a Journey: A Road Map for Spiritual Formation.* Downers Grove, IL: InterVarsity Press, 2016.

Mulrain, George. "The Use of the Senses in Worship." *Caribbean Journal of Religious Studies* 17/2 (1996): 32–38.

Nash, Robert N., Jr. *Moving the Equator: The Families of the Earth and the Mission of the Church.* Macon, GA: Smyth & Helwys, 2020. Kindle edition.

NICM Health Research Institute, Western Sydney University. "How the Internet May be Changing the Brain." *ScienceDaily.* June 5, 2019. sciencedaily.com/releases/2019/06/190605100345.htm.

Olson, Dennis T. "Sacred Time: The Sabbath and Christian Worship." *Touching the Altar: The Old Testament for Christian Worship*, ed. Carol M. Bechtel. Grand Rapids: Eerdmans, 2008. Kindle edition.

Penner, Carol. "Congregational Prayer—For Palm Sunday." *Common Word.* 2012. commonword.ca/ResourceView/82/21783.

Pitzele, Peter A. *Scripture Windows: Toward a Practice of Bibliodrama.* Los Angeles: Torah Aura Productions, 1998.

Plantinga, Cornelius, Jr. and Sue A. Rozeboom. *Discerning the Spirits: A Guide to Thinking about Christian Worship Today.* Grand Rapids: Eerdmans, 2003.

Rainer, Thom S. *The Post-Quarantine Church: Six Urgent Challenges and Opportunities That Will Determine the Future of Your Congregation.* Tyndale House Publishers, Inc., 2020. Kindle edition.

"Religion in America: U.S. Religious Data, Demographics and Statistics." Pew Research Center's Religion & Public Life Project, September 9, 2020. pewforum.org/religious-landscape-study/attendance-at-religious-services/.

Rhor, Richard. "Between Two Worlds." *Center for Action and Contemplation.* April 27, 2020. https://cac.org/between-two-worlds-2020-04-26/.

———. "Loving the Presence in the Present." *Center for Action and Contemplation.* 29 December 2015. https://cac.org/loving-the-presence-in-the-present-2015-12-29/.

Scharen, Christian. *Fieldwork in Theology: The Church and Postmodern Culture.* Grand Rapids: Baker Publishing Group, 2015. Kindle edition.

Schmit, Clayton J. *Too Deep for Words: A Theology of Liturgical Expression.* Louisville: Westminster John Knox Press, 2002.

Schreiter, Robert J. *Constructing Local Theologies.* Maryknoll, NY: Orbis Books, 2001.

Segler, Franklin M. *Understanding, Preparing for, and Practicing Christian Worship.* Nashville: Broadman & Holman Publishers, 1996.

Sensing, Tim. *Qualitative Research: A Multi-Methods Approach to Projects for Doctor of Ministry Theses.* Eugene, OR: Wipf & Stock, 2011. Kindle edition.

Smith, James K. A. *Awaiting the King: Reforming Public Theology.* Grand Rapids: Baker Publishing Group, 2017.

———. *Desiring the Kingdom: Worship, Worldview, and Cultural Formation.* Grand Rapids: Baker Publishing Group, 2009.

———. *Imagining the Kingdom: How Worship Works.* Grand Rapids: Baker Publishing Group, 2013.

Taylor, Charles. *A Secular Age.* Cambridge, MA: The Belknap Press of Harvard University Press, 2007.

Thomas, Gary. *Sacred Pathways: Discover Your Soul's Path to God.* Grand Rapids: Zondervan, 2010.

"Transliteration." *Vocabulary.* Thinkmap, Inc., 1998–2021. vocabulary.com/dictionary/transliteration.

Tucker, Karen B. Westerfield. "North America." *The Oxford History of Christian Worship.* Oxford: Oxford University Press, 2006.

United Methodist Church. Discipleship Ministries. A Service of Tenebrae. umcdiscipleship.org/resources/a-service-of-tenebrae.

Van Dyk, Leanne, ed. *A More Profound Alleluia: Theology and Worship in Harmony.* Grand Rapids: Eerdmans, 2005.

Warren, Tish Harrison. *Liturgy of the Ordinary.* Downers Grove, IL: InterVarsity Press, 2016.

Wettstein, Howard. *The Significance of Religious Experience.* Oxford: Oxford University Press, 2012.

White, James F. *Introduction to Christian Worship.* Nashville: Abingdon Press, 2000.

————. "The Spatial Setting." *The Oxford History of Christian Worship.* Oxford: Oxford University Press, 2006.

White, Susan J. *Foundations of Christian Worship.* Louisville: Westminster John Knox Press, 2006.

Witvliet, John D. *The Biblical Psalms in Christian Worship.* Grand Rapids: Eerdmans, 2007.

————. "The Opening of Worship: Trinity." *A More Profound Alleluia.* Grand Rapids: Eerdmans, 2005.

————. *Worship Seeking Understanding: Windows into Christian Practice.* Grand Rapids: Eerdmans, 2003.

Wright, N. T. *God and the Pandemic.* Grand Rapids: Zondervan, 2020. Kindle edition.

————. *Surprised by Hope: Rethinking Heaven, the Resurrection, and the Mission of the Church.* New York: HarperOne, 2008.

ENDNOTES

1. Thom S. Rainer, *The Post-Quarantine Church: Six Urgent Challenges and Opportunities that Will Determine the Future of Your Congregation* (Kindle ed.; Carol Stream, IL: Tyndale House Publishers, Inc., 2020), 26.

2. "In the same way, the Spirit also helps us in our weakness, since we do not know how to pray as we should. But the Spirit himself intercedes for us with groans too deep for words . . ." (Rom 8:26, International Standard Version).

3. Joel Clarkson, *Sensing God: Experiencing the Divine in Nature, Food, Music, and Beauty* (Kindle ed.; Carol Stream, IL: NavPress, 2021), 5.

4. Søren Kierkegaard, *Purity of Heart Is to Will One Thing* (New York: Simon and Schuster, 2013), 147.

5. Ruth C. Duck, *Worship for the Whole People of God: Vital Worship for the 21st Century* (Louisville: Westminster John Knox Press, 2013), 7–14; John E. Burkhart, *Worship: A Searching Examination of the Liturgical Experience* (Philadelphia: Westminster Press, 1982), 31–33, quoted in Duck, *Worship for the Whole People of God*, 7–14.

6. "Transliteration is the process of transferring a word from the alphabet of one language to the alphabet of another. Transliteration helps people pronounce words and names in foreign languages. Unlike a translation, which tells you the meaning of a word that's written in another language, a transliteration only gives you an idea of how the word is pronounced by putting it in a familiar alphabet. It changes the letters from the word's original alphabet to similar-sounding letters in a different one. In Hebrew, the Jewish winter holiday is חנוכה. Its English

transliteration is Hanukkah or Chanukah." ("Transliteration," *Vocabulary. com*, vocabulary.com/dictionary/transliteration).

7. Chip Heath and Dan Heath, *The Power of Moments: Why Certain Experiences Have Extraordinary Impact* (Kindle ed.; Simon & Schuster, 2017), 7.

8. "Livestream" means to broadcast over the internet, whether on YouTube or some other medium.

9. Heath and Heath, *The Power of Moments*, 216.

10. "The better you are at combining visual and auditory information, the better you can remember what you've learned. This conclusion reached by neuroscientists at UNIL demonstrates the effectiveness of teaching methods which simultaneously make use of multiple senses, like that developed by Maria Montessori" (Elisabeth Gordon, "Using Multiple Senses to Improve Memory, Université de Lausanne (UNIL), https://wp.unil.ch/discoverunil/2016/11/using-multiple-senses-to-im-prove-memory/#:~:text=Yet%20the%20neuroscientist%20points%20 out,remember%20what%20you've%20learned).

11. For a complete explanation of this concept, see the "Intermezzo" introduction to Part 2 of Alan J. Roxburgh's book *Missional* (Kindle ed.; Baker Publishing Group, 2011), 57.

12. Both quoted in Roxburgh, *Missional*, 57.

13. Ibid., 166.

14. Ibid., 60–61.

15. Ibid., 61.

16. For an in-depth discussion of these perspectives, see W. Paul Jones, *Theological Worlds: Understanding the Alternative Rhythms of Christian Belief* (Nashville: Abingdon Press, 1989).

17. "Liturgy" refers to the order in which you structure your worship service. If you have a welcome, three praise and worship songs by the band, a video, and a sermon, that's still a liturgy!

18. James F. White, *Introduction to Christian Worship*, 3rd ed. (Nashville: Abingdon, 2000), 31.

19. Duck, *Worship for the Whole People of God*, 4.

20. See Martien A. Halvorson-Taylor, "Exile in the Hebrew Bible," Bible Odyssey, bibleodyssey.org/en/places/related-articles/exile-in-the-hebrew-bible.

21. Roxburgh, *Missional*, 173.

22. I based the service around "A Service of Tenebrae," UMCDiscipleship, November 10, 2014. Accessed April 13, 2021, umcdiscipleship.org/resources/a-service-of-tenebrae.

23. A version of this video service can be found at sensinggodonline.com.

24. Duck, *Worship for the Whole People of God*, 5.

25. Erin Tierman, "Churches linked to dozens of coronavirus clusters in Massachusetts, but no new restrictions coming," *Boston Herald*, December 1, 2020; Kaitlin McKinley Becker, "More Than 200 COVID-19 Cases Linked to Fitchburg Church," NBCBoston.com, nbcboston.com/news/local/more-than-200-covid-19-cases-linked-to-fitchburg-church/2225433/?amp; Alison Kuznitz, "More COVID-19 deaths linked to super-spreader event at Charlotte church," *Charlotte Observer*, November 4, 2020.

26. Ashlin-Mayo, *Digital Mission*, 8.

27. Ibid., 54.

28. Ibid., 8.

29. Kep Pate, in discussion with the author, January 7, 2021.

30. Ibid.

31. "Religion in America: U.S. Religious Data, Demographics and Statistics," Pew Research Center's Religion & Public Life Project, September 9, 2020, pewforum.org/religious-landscape-study/attendance-at-religious-services/.

32. Richard Rhor, "Loving the Presence in the Present," Center for Action and Contemplation, December 29, 2015, cac.org/loving-the-presence-in-the-present-2015-12-29/.

33. Aidan Kavanagh quoted in Schmit, *Too Deep*, 39.

34. Ibid., 39.

35. N. T. Wright, *God and the Pandemic* (Grand Rapids: Zondervan, 2020), Kindle edition, 68.

36. Gerard Manley Hopkins, "God's Grandeur," public domain text available atpoetryfoundation.org/poems/44395/gods-grandeur.

37. The information in this section is adapted from Joseph Campbell's *The Hero with A Thousand Faces*, 3rd ed. (San Francisco: New World Library, 2008), Kindle edition.

38. Please note that this is easier to accomplish with a prerecorded service. Some livestreams can be paused while others cannot. Determine which you are using, and if pausing is not an option, try to communicate the task ahead of time with your weekly announcements so that worshipers will be prepared with the necessary physical elements.

39. The quote "The cave you fear to enter holds the treasure you seek" is commonly attributed to Joseph Campbell but may be apocryphal. The same sentiment is echoed in the works of Carl Jung: "The process of individuation, a fundamental psychological and life-process by which a person integrates disparate parts of their self into a whole, acknowledges the fact that the individual must engage all aspects of who they are, even those which they fear" (Scott Myers, "Wisdom on creativity from Joseph Campbell and Carl Jung," Go into the Story, gointothestory.blcklst.com/the-cave-you-fear-to-enter-holds-the-treasure-you-seek-d624e28c3848).

40. Cyndi Parr, email to the author, January 12, 2021.

41. "[T]he most important symbol in Grace Church [is] not the cross or the altar or any of that, but the sign at the back of the church saying EXIT in glowing red—that's what all that happens in the church is for" (Michael McCann, email to the author, March 18, 2020).

42. Dr. David G. Garber, Jr., email to the author, January 19, 2021.

43. Gary A. Furr and Milburn Price, *The Dialogue of Worship: Creating Space for Revelation and Response* (Macon, GA: Smyth & Helwys, 1998), 2.

44. Ibid., 2–3.

45. Ibid., 3.

46. Witvliet, "Opening of Worship," 15.

47. See Søren Kierkegaard, *Purity of Heart Is to Will One Thing* (New York: Simon & Schuster, 2013).

48. In *Touching the Altar*, ed. Bechtel, Kindle loc. 188–91.

49. T. C. Smith, *Beyond the Shadows: Embracing Authentic Worship* (Macon, GA: Smyth & Helwys, 2000), 2.

50. Ibid., 2.

51. See Ruth C. Duck's *Worship for the Whole People of God: Vital Worship for the 21st Century* (Louisville: Westminster John Knox, 2013), 3–5.

52. In *Touching the Altar*, ed. Bechtel, Kindle loc. 312.

53. Olson, "Sacred Time," in *Touching the Altar*, ed. Bechtel, Kindle loc. 296–98.

54. jewishwikipedia.info/movement_babylon.html.

55. Dr. David G. Garber, Jr., email to the author, January 19, 2021.

56. David R. Kirk, "When You Come Together: Gathered Worship in the New Testament," *Foundations* (Affinity) 76 (Spring 2019): 34–60.

57. Robert N. Nash, Jr., *Moving the Equator: The Families of the Earth and the Mission of the Church* (Macon, GA: Smyth & Helwys, 2020), Kindle edition, 30.

58. Bryce Ashlin-Mayo, *Digital Mission: A Practical Guide for Ministry Online* (Toronto: Tyndale Academic Press, 2020), Kindle edition, 54.

59. Nash, *Moving the Equator*, 139–40.

60. Kirk, "When You Come Together," 43.

61. Ibid.

62. Ibid., 50.

63. Ralph P. Martin, "New Testament Worship: Some Puzzling Practices," *Andrews University Seminary Studies* 31/2 (Summer 1993): 119–26.

64. Gerald L. Borchert, "The Lord of Form and Freedom: A New Testament Perspective on Worship," *Review & Expositor* 80/1 (Winter 1983): 5–18.

65. Robert N. Nash, Jr., "Divine Encounters," sermon delivered at Heritage Fellowship in Canton, Georgia, on April 18, 2021.

66. Shaun King, pastor of Johns Creek Baptist Church, interview by author, October 22, 2020, Zoom teleconference video recording, Johns Creek Baptist Church, Alpharetta, Georgia.

67. C. S. Lewis, *Mere Christianity* (New York: Touchstone, 1943), 143, quoted in John D. Witvliet, "The Opening of Worship: Trinity," *A More Profound Alleluia* (Grand Rapids: Eerdmans, 2005), 2.

68. Witvliet, "The Opening of Worship: Trinity," 2.

69. James K. A. Smith, *Desiring the Kingdom: Worship, Worldview, and Cultural Formation* (Grand Rapids: Baker Publishing Group, 2009), 33.

70. Charles Taylor, *A Secular Age* (Cambridge, MA: The Belknap Press of Harvard University Press, 2007), 2.

71. Smith, *Desiring the Kingdom*, 40.

72. Ibid., 62–63.

73. Clayton J. Schmit, *Too Deep for Words: A Theology of Liturgical Expression* (Louisville: Westminster John Knox, 2002), 31. Here, Schmit reverts to the old French root of the word that means "to carry through to completion."

74. Ibid., 31.

75. Ibid., 33.

76. St. Thomas Aquinas, *Summa Theologiae: A Concise Translation*, ed. Timothy McDermott (Allen, TX: Christian Classics, 1989), 300–301.

77. Ibid., 547.

78. Duck, *Worship for the Whole People of God*, 79.

79. Ibid., 79–80.

80. Ibid., 90.

81. Dom Gregory Dix, *The Shape of the Liturgy* (London: Bloomsbury, 2005), 161–62.

82. Ibid., 263.

83. Jacob M. Baum, *Reformation of the Senses, Studies in Sensory History* (Springfield: University of Illinois Press, 2019), Kindle edition, 254.

84. Nathan D. Mitchell, "Reforms, Protestant and Catholic," *The Oxford History of Christian Worship* (Oxford: Oxford University Press, 2006), 319.

85. Ibid., 318.

86. Ibid., 320.

87. Baum, *Reformation of the Senses*, 354.

88. Karen B. Westerfield Tucker, "North America," *The Oxford History of Christian Worship* (Oxford: Oxford University Press, 2006), 596–97.

89. Ibid., 597.

90. Fanny Crosby, "Blessed Assurance," *Palmer's Guide to Holiness and Revival Miscellany*, July 1873, 36.

91. BGEA, "A Look Back at Billy Graham's Largest Ever Crusade," Billy Graham Evangelistic Association, June 3, 2019, billygraham.org/story/seoul-south-korea-a-look-back-at-billy-grahams-largest-ever-crusade.

92. Tucker, "North America," 627.

93. Ibid., 607.

94. James F. White, "The Spatial Setting," *The Oxford History of Christian Worship* (Oxford: Oxford University Press, 2006), 803.

95. Ibid., 806.

96. "Professor Jerome Sarris, Deputy Director and Director of Research at NICM Health Research Institute, Western Sydney University and senior author on the report, is concerned over some of the potential impacts of increasing Internet use on the brain. 'The bombardment of stimuli via the Internet, and the resultant divided attention commonly experienced, presents a range of concerns,' said Professor Sarris. 'I believe that this, along with the increasing #Instagramification of society, has the ability to alter both the structure and functioning of the brain, while potentially also altering our social fabric'" (NICM Health Research Institute, Western Sydney University, "How the Internet May Be Changing the Brain," *ScienceDaily,* June 5, 2019, sciencedaily.com/releases/2019/06/190605100345.htm.

97. It's a common misconception that church prayer requests can violate HIPAA (American Health Insurance Portability and Accountability Act of 1996), but the act does not apply to churches. Still, it's important to respect members' privacy regarding any sensitive or health-related information that's disseminated online or in any other format. See Mike Greer, "HIPPA [*sic*] and church prayer requests," September 24, 2014, baptistnews.com/article/hippa-and-church-prayer-requests/ for a helpful guide.

98. "Breaking the script means to violate expectations about an experience" (Chip Heath and Dan Heath, *The Power of Moments: Why Certain Experiences Have Extraordinary Impact* [New York: Simon & Schuster, 2017], Kindle Edition, 61).

99. A "hashtag" is a word or brief phrase with # in front of it, and it's used to find related content on social media. Click on a hashtag, and it displays other posts that have used the same tag. Using a unique tag for your church (ours is #HolyHealthyWhole) will allow social media users to easily access everything that has been said by your group about that topic.

100. The numbers of views and other statistics related your content are collectively known as "analytics," and this information can be accessed in a variety of ways based on your content platform. Check SensingGodOnline.com for more details about how to access this information.

101. 1 Thess 5:19, NRSV.

102. Duck, *Worship for the Whole People of God*, 3–5.

103. Kep Pate, in discussion with the author, January 7, 2021.

104. Richard Rohr, "Between Two Worlds," Center for Action and Contemplation, April 27, 2020, cac.org/between-two-worlds-2020-04-26.